The Art of Communicating with Preteens

Marcia Williams

Dedication

This book is dedicated to all parents of preteens—the unsung heroes who navigate the complexities of this challenging yet rewarding stage with unwavering love, patience, and resilience. Your dedication to understanding and connecting with your children, even amidst the hormonal rollercoasters, the social pressures, and the evolving dynamics of family life, is truly inspirational. This work is a small token of appreciation for your tireless efforts in building strong and lasting relationships with your preteens, fostering their growth, and shaping their futures. Your commitment to nurturing their development and providing a safe and supportive environment is the bedrock of a healthy family dynamic, and your love and understanding are the most powerful tools you possess. May this guide empower you further in your journey, helping you build even stronger bonds of connection with your child. To the parents who seek to cultivate understanding, communication, and unwavering support: this is for you.

Preface

The preteen years—a bridge between childhood and adolescence—are a period of remarkable transformation. Physically, cognitively, and emotionally, your child undergoes significant changes that can impact their behavior, communication style, and relationships with family and friends. For parents, this can be a time of both joy and frustration, marked by shifting dynamics and communication challenges. This book, "Communicating with Preteens," is designed to be your compass, guiding you through the often turbulent waters of this pivotal developmental stage.

It provides practical strategies and insightful perspectives, empowering you to understand your child's unique needs and build stronger, healthier connections. Drawing upon current research in child psychology and backed by real-life examples, this guide offers a supportive and empathetic approach to improving communication with your preteen. It acknowledges the complexities of the preteen mind and provides actionable advice that you can immediately implement in your daily interactions. Remember, effective communication is not just about talking; it's about listening, understanding, and fostering a genuine connection. This book serves as your guide on that journey, empowering you to build a stronger, more meaningful relationship with your child. It's a journey of growth and understanding – for both you and your preteen.

Introduction

The preteen years (ages 9-12) mark a significant transition in a child's life, a period characterized by rapid physical, cognitive, and emotional development. This stage often presents unique communication challenges for parents, as children navigate the complexities of their changing identities, peer relationships, and academic pressures. Misunderstandings and conflict can easily arise if parents fail to recognize and adapt to these evolving needs. "Communicating with Preteens" offers a comprehensive and practical guide to help parents bridge this communication gap and foster strong, lasting relationships with their children. This book is not a simple manual of instructions but rather an empathetic companion on your parenting journey. We will delve into the science behind preteen development, examining the biological, psychological, and social factors that influence their behavior and communication styles. This understanding will empower you to respond to challenges with sensitivity and effective strategies, transforming potentially tense situations into opportunities for growth and connection. We will explore proven techniques for active listening, setting healthy boundaries, and resolving conflicts respectfully. The book addresses specific challenges parents commonly face, including managing academic pressures, navigating the complexities of peer relationships and social media, and handling sibling rivalry and family conflicts. Each chapter provides practical, actionable advice coupled with real-life examples to illustrate the concepts discussed. More importantly, "Communicating with Preteens" emphasizes building a positive and supportive relationship based on mutual respect, trust, and open communication — a foundation that will benefit your child throughout their life. We'll explore ways to create routines and rituals that foster connection and provide opportunities for open dialogue, even in the midst of busy schedules. Finally, we acknowledge that parenting is not a solo journey. The book will highlight the importance of seeking professional help when necessary and provides resources to support you along the way. This is your guide to navigating this crucial developmental stage, building stronger connections, and fostering a positive, healthy family life.

Chapter 1
Understanding the Preteen Mind

T he preteen years, spanning roughly from ages nine to twelve, represent a pivotal developmental stage characterized by significant physical, cognitive, and emotional transformations. Understanding these changes is crucial for parents seeking to effectively communicate with and support their children during this period. This period marks a bridge between childhood and adolescence, a transition often fraught with challenges and uncertainties for both parents and children.

Physically, preteens are experiencing a surge in growth and development, often leading to awkwardness and self-consciousness. Girls may experience the onset of puberty earlier than boys, leading to a disparity in physical maturity and potentially impacting their social interactions and self-esteem. This physical development can be accompanied by fluctuating hormone levels, contributing to mood swings, increased irritability, and emotional volatility. These hormonal shifts are not simply a matter of "teenage hormones"; they are real biological changes impacting brain function and emotional regulation, making it crucial for parents to understand their influence on behavior. Parents should anticipate these changes and be prepared to provide support and understanding, rather than reacting with frustration or criticism. Openly discussing these changes, using age-appropriate language, can help demystify the process and reduce anxiety.

Cognitively, preteens are undergoing significant advancements in their thinking abilities. While still concrete in their thinking, they are beginning to develop more abstract reasoning skills. This allows them to grapple with more complex ideas and concepts, but it also means they are increasingly aware of their own thoughts and feelings, as well as the perspectives of others. This developing metacognition—the ability to think about thinking—can lead to introspection, self-doubt, and a heightened awareness of social dynamics. Their increased cognitive capacity also allows them to engage in more sophisticated problem-solving, but this newfound ability may not always translate into improved decision-making, particularly when navigating social pressures or emotional challenges. Patience and guidance are key during this period, allowing preteens the space to develop their cognitive skills while providing support when needed.

Emotionally, the preteen years are a time of intense exploration and self-discovery. Preteens are grappling with their developing sense of self and identity, exploring their values, beliefs, and interests. They are increasingly seeking independence and autonomy, yet they still require parental guidance and support. This can lead to conflict as they attempt to assert their independence while grappling with their need for security and reassurance. This push for independence often manifests as defiance, arguing, and a reluctance to follow parental rules. It is important to remember that this isn't necessarily a rejection of parents, but a natural part of their developmental journey toward self-reliance. Understanding this fundamental shift helps parents respond more effectively and avoid unnecessary conflict. Providing opportunities for age-appropriate independence while establishing clear and consistent boundaries is crucial for fostering both autonomy and security.

The developing sense of self is significantly impacted by peer relationships. During the preteen years, peer groups take on increasing importance, influencing everything from fashion choices and social behavior to attitudes and values. This peer influence can be both positive and negative, depending on the dynamics of the peer group and the individual's level of self-esteem. Preteens who lack a strong sense of self may be more susceptible to negative peer pressure, engaging in risky behaviors or adopting values that conflict with those of their parents. Strong communication between parents and children is critical in navigating these social waters. Openly discussing social situations, addressing peer pressure directly, and fostering open dialogue can help preteens develop the critical thinking skills necessary to make healthy choices and build positive relationships.

The brain undergoes significant structural and functional changes during preadolescence. Research using neuroimaging techniques has revealed significant development in the prefrontal cortex, the area of the brain responsible for executive functions such as planning, decision-making, and impulse control. However, this area of the brain is not fully developed during preadolescence, making it challenging for preteens to regulate their emotions, control impulses, and think critically in emotionally charged situations. This means that while they are capable of abstract thought and complex reasoning, they may struggle to apply these skills consistently, especially when under stress or emotional pressure. This explains why seemingly rational decisions can be overshadowed by impulsive actions or emotional responses. Parents should be aware of these limitations and respond accordingly, focusing on empathy, understanding, and providing age-appropriate guidance rather than punishment.

The impact of these developmental changes extends to the parent-child relationship. What worked in communication with a younger child may be completely ineffective with a preteen. Parents need to adapt their communication styles to meet their child's evolving needs and abilities. This means moving beyond simple directives and engaging in more nuanced and reciprocal conversations. Active listening, empathy, and respect are crucial for building trust and fostering open communication. Parents need to be mindful of their own communication styles, ensuring that they are not overly critical, dismissive, or controlling. Creating a safe and supportive environment where preteens feel comfortable expressing their thoughts and feelings, even when those thoughts and feelings differ from the parents', is essential for maintaining a healthy relationship.

Furthermore, the increased independence sought by preteens often leads to conflicts over rules and expectations. Setting clear and consistent boundaries is crucial, but these boundaries should be age-appropriate and explained with reasoning. Simply stating a rule without providing context or rationale can lead to resentment and defiance. Involving preteens in the process of setting rules and expectations can foster a sense of responsibility and ownership. This doesn't mean allowing children to dictate the rules, but rather incorporating their input in a way that demonstrates respect for their opinions and growing independence.

The preteen years are a time of significant transitions and challenges, but they are also a time of incredible growth and development. By understanding the unique developmental stage of preteens, parents can effectively communicate with their children, fostering a strong and healthy relationship that supports their journey toward adulthood. Remember, patience, empathy, and clear communication are key to navigating this complex and crucial period in a child's life. Openly discussing the changes that both parent and child are going through will foster a bond of understanding that can strengthen the family unit and help children navigate this often confusing and turbulent period. Regular family time, consistent routine, and a willingness to listen and understand will go a long way in creating a positive and supportive environment where preteens can flourish. Seeking professional guidance when needed is not a sign of failure, but rather a testament to a parent's commitment to their child's well-being.

Effective communication with preteens requires navigating a complex landscape of developmental changes and evolving relationships. One of the primary hurdles is the significant generational gap that can exist between parents and their preteen children. Parents, often raised in a different era with different social norms and technological advancements, may struggle to understand the perspectives and experiences of their children. This disconnect can manifest in various ways, from differing opinions on appropriate clothing and music to differing views on social media use and screen time. The language used by each generation can also be a barrier, with slang and internet-speak creating a communication chasm. A parent unfamiliar with the nuances of their child's online world may find it difficult to engage meaningfully in conversations about their digital life. Understanding the cultural context of their child's peer group is also crucial to bridge this gap. Parents can proactively bridge this generational divide by making an effort to understand their child's world, engaging in their interests, and actively listening to their perspectives, even when those perspectives differ significantly. Actively engaging with their music, social media, or games can provide insights into their social circles and cultural references, demonstrating interest and understanding. It is equally important for preteens to appreciate that their parents have different experiences and backgrounds.

Hormonal changes during preadolescence significantly contribute to communication challenges. The fluctuating hormone levels associated with puberty can cause dramatic mood swings, irritability, and emotional volatility. These are not simply "teenage hormones" but are driven by real biological changes in the brain that affect emotional regulation and impulse control. A preteen's sudden outburst of anger or extreme sadness is often a manifestation of these hormonal fluctuations, not necessarily a reflection of their feelings towards their parents or a deliberate attempt to be difficult. Parents must approach these emotional outbursts with empathy and understanding, recognizing that their child's reactions are often beyond their conscious control. Avoid reacting defensively or engaging in arguments during these emotionally charged moments. Instead, wait until the child has calmed down before attempting to address the underlying issues. Providing a safe space for the child to express their feelings without judgment is crucial. Emphasizing that it's okay to feel a range of emotions and validating their feelings, even when their behavior is challenging, can help build trust and encourage open communication. Learning to recognize the triggers for their child's emotional outbursts can also help parents to anticipate and potentially mitigate future conflicts. This might involve paying attention to diet, sleep patterns, stress levels, and social situations that exacerbate these emotional fluctuations.

The preteen's growing desire for independence presents another major communication barrier. Preteens are increasingly assertive about their autonomy, seeking to make their own choices and express their individuality. This is a natural part of their development, a crucial step in their journey towards self-reliance and adulthood. However, this drive for independence often manifests as defiance of parental rules, reluctance to follow instructions, and an overall resistance to authority. This is not necessarily a rejection of parents but an expression of their evolving sense of self and their need to assert control over their lives. Parents must understand this developmental shift and adjust their approach accordingly. Avoid authoritarian responses; instead, focus on collaborative decision-making and open dialogue. Giving preteens age-appropriate choices and opportunities for independence will help them feel empowered and reduce their need to rebel. For instance, allowing a child to choose their own clothes (within reasonable limits), manage their own time for homework, or participate in extracurricular activities they are passionate about can foster their sense of autonomy. Setting clear and consistent boundaries is essential, but parents should strive to explain the reasoning behind those rules, involving their children in the decision-making process whenever possible. This demonstrates respect for their opinions and builds a sense of shared responsibility. Openly communicating expectations and consequences also reinforces boundaries and limits.

The increasing influence of peers adds another layer of complexity to communication. During the preteen years, peer relationships become increasingly important, often shaping a child's attitudes, values, and behaviors. Preteens may be influenced by their friends' opinions on everything from clothing and music to social norms and academic performance. This peer influence can be both positive and negative, depending on the values and behaviors modeled within their social groups. Children might adopt slang, styles of clothing, or behaviors that are at odds with their family values. They may engage in risky behaviors or make decisions that they wouldn't otherwise consider in an effort to fit in or gain acceptance from their peers. Parents must not only understand this powerful influence but also work to support their children in navigating the social pressures they face. This requires actively listening to their child's social experiences, fostering open dialogue about peer relationships, and collaboratively establishing guidelines for safe and responsible social interactions. Focusing on the importance of healthy friendships, critical thinking skills, and decision-making will empower the preteen to make informed choices. Discussing current events, movies, television shows, books, or music can open avenues of communication and provide opportunities to address social issues and values.

Technology adds another substantial layer to communication challenges. The prevalence of smartphones, social media, and online gaming has fundamentally altered the way preteens interact with the world, their friends, and their family. This increased screen time can lead to communication difficulties, as preteens may withdraw from face-to-face interactions, spending more time in their online spaces. Moreover, parental concerns about cyberbullying, online safety, and appropriate technology use often create conflicts. Open communication about online behavior, potential risks, and responsible technology usage is crucial. Setting clear boundaries around screen time, monitoring online activity, and engaging in conversations about online safety are important components of parenting in the digital age. Parents need to learn how to navigate this digital landscape effectively and engage in meaningful conversations with their children about their online experiences. This may involve learning about the social media platforms their children use, familiarizing themselves with online games and trends, and fostering open communication about online safety and appropriate online behavior.

The complexities of school and academic pressures also affect communication. Preteens face increasing academic demands, potentially leading to stress, anxiety, and frustration. The pressure to perform well academically, coupled with the social pressures of school, can lead to difficulties in communicating feelings of stress or academic challenges. Open conversations about academic struggles, goals, and study habits are crucial. Parents should create an environment where their preteens feel comfortable sharing their academic successes and failures, without judgment. This means avoiding pressure-filled conversations about grades, focusing instead on creating a supportive and encouraging atmosphere for learning. Actively engaging with their schoolwork and fostering a positive attitude towards learning can significantly improve communication during this challenging period. This could involve assisting with homework, attending school events, and helping them develop effective study habits. Recognizing the signs of stress, such as changes in sleep patterns, irritability, or withdrawn behavior, is essential to provide support and guidance.

Finally, parental communication styles can significantly impact the effectiveness of communication with preteens. Parents who utilize an authoritarian approach, characterized by rigid rules and strict enforcement without explanation, are likely to experience more conflict and less open communication. Conversely, overly permissive parenting styles can lead to a lack of boundaries and structure, resulting in communication difficulties. The most effective approach involves a balanced style of parenting that incorporates clear boundaries with open communication and empathy. This approach acknowledges the preteen's growing need for autonomy while maintaining parental guidance and support. Parents must consciously work on their listening skills, employing active listening techniques such as maintaining eye contact, providing verbal and non-verbal cues of understanding, and reflecting back what their child has shared. Avoiding interrupting, judging, or offering unsolicited advice will encourage open communication. Showing empathy and validating their feelings, even when disagreeing with their behavior, is essential in fostering a trusting relationship.

In conclusion, effective communication with preteens requires understanding the complex interplay of developmental changes, social influences, technological advancements, and family dynamics. By acknowledging the common communication barriers, parents can develop strategies to foster open dialogue, build trust, and maintain a strong and supportive relationship with their children during this pivotal stage of their lives. Remembering that preteens are navigating significant changes and challenges requires patience, empathy, and a willingness to adapt communication styles to meet their evolving needs. This commitment to understanding and open communication will strengthen the family bond and provide essential support as preteens transition towards adolescence and adulthood.

Active listening is more than just hearing what your preteen says; it's about truly understanding their perspective, their emotions, and the unspoken messages conveyed through their body language. This is crucial during the preteen years, a period marked by significant emotional fluctuations and a developing sense of self. Their words may only tell part of the story; the rest is often communicated through subtle nonverbal cues – a slumped posture, a fleeting glance away, a clenched fist – that can speak volumes about their inner state. Learning to recognize and interpret these cues is the first step towards truly effective communication.

For example, a preteen might say, "It's fine," while simultaneously exhibiting furrowed brows, crossed arms, and a flat tone of voice. The words suggest nonchalance, but the body language screams frustration or hurt. Ignoring the nonverbal cues and focusing solely on the words could lead to a misunderstanding, potentially widening the communication gap. Instead, validating the nonverbal cues by saying something like, "You say it's fine, but you seem a little upset. Can we talk about it?" opens the door for honest and open communication.

Validating feelings is paramount. Preteens, undergoing significant hormonal and emotional shifts, often struggle to understand and process their own feelings. They may express anger, sadness, or frustration in ways that seem disproportionate to the situation. Rather than dismissing these emotions or minimizing their experiences, validate their feelings by acknowledging their emotional state. For instance, if your preteen is upset about a conflict with a friend, a response like, "That sounds really frustrating. It must be tough to feel like that," demonstrates empathy and creates a safe space for them to open up. Avoid using phrases like "You shouldn't feel that way" or "Just get over it," as these statements invalidate their emotions and shut down communication.

Responding appropriately without judgment is another critical aspect of active listening. During emotionally charged moments, the tendency is to react defensively or offer unsolicited advice. However, preteens need to feel heard and understood before they are ready to accept guidance. Instead of jumping to solutions, focus on reflecting their feelings. For instance, if they are complaining about a difficult assignment, a response like, "So, you're feeling overwhelmed by the amount of work and the pressure to get good grades?" allows them to process their feelings before seeking solutions together. Avoid interrupting or offering quick fixes; let them fully express themselves before intervening.

Summarizing their points is a powerful active listening technique, particularly in longer or more complex conversations. This shows that you've been paying attention and reinforces your understanding. After your preteen has shared their concerns, briefly summarize their main points, allowing them to correct any misunderstandings or add further details. This also demonstrates your engagement and encourages them to continue the dialogue.

Reframing their perspective is a more advanced technique that can help preteens see their situations differently and manage challenging emotions. It doesn't mean dismissing their feelings; instead, it involves gently guiding them towards a more balanced perspective. If a preteen is convinced they failed a test because they are simply not smart, you could gently reframe it by acknowledging their frustration while emphasizing their hard work and suggesting strategies to improve. For example, you could say, "I understand you're feeling discouraged about the test, but you've worked really hard, and there are other ways to approach studying that could help. Perhaps we can try a different study method or talk to your teacher?" The focus here is on helping them learn from the situation rather than dwelling on perceived failures.

Let's explore some practical scenarios to illustrate these techniques:

Scenario 1: The Angry Outburst

Your preteen slams their bedroom door after receiving a less-than-stellar grade on a history test. Instead of reacting with anger or lecturing them about responsibility, approach them calmly. You could say, "I heard the door slam. You seem really upset about the history test. Can you tell me what's going on?" This demonstrates empathy and invites them to open up. Once they explain, you can validate their feelings, saying, "That sounds really frustrating. It's okay to feel disappointed when things don't go as planned." You can then summarize their main point, "So, you feel the test was unfair, and you're worried about your grade in history." Finally, you can gently reframe their perspective, "While the test might have been challenging, it doesn't reflect your overall abilities in history. We can work together to create a study plan for the next test."

Scenario 2: The Silent Treatment

Your preteen has been unusually quiet and withdrawn after spending time with their friends. Instead of pushing them to talk, try to create a comfortable environment. You might approach them while engaging in a shared activity, saying, "You seem quiet today. Is something bothering you?" This creates an opportunity for conversation without pressure. If they remain silent, respect their space, but let them know you're there for them when they're ready to talk. If they do open up about a conflict with a friend, focus on listening attentively and validating their feelings. Avoid offering immediate solutions, instead reflecting back their emotions, "So you feel betrayed by your friend's actions, and that's causing you a lot of hurt." Summarize their key concerns and then help them explore solutions, rather than offering advice directly.

Scenario 3: The Technology Struggle

Your preteen is constantly on their phone and seems to be ignoring family conversations. Instead of scolding them or confiscating their phone, approach the situation calmly. Begin by saying, "I've noticed you've been spending a lot of time on your phone lately, and I'm a little worried we're not connecting as much as we used to. Is everything okay?" This opens a dialogue about the issue without resorting to blame. If they admit that they are spending too much time on their phone and they miss out on family moments, acknowledge their feelings, "That sounds like it is difficult, you're missing time with your family that you value." Summarize their perspective, "You want to be on your phone, but you also wish you weren't missing out on family time." Then, work collaboratively to establish healthy boundaries, involving them in the decision-making process.

Remember, active listening is not a one-size-fits-all approach. It requires adapting your style to your preteen's individual personality and communication style. Some preteens might respond best to direct questions, while others might prefer subtle cues and open-ended prompts. The key is to be patient, empathetic, and genuinely interested in understanding their perspective. By mastering the art of active listening and empathetic communication, parents can build stronger relationships with their preteens, fostering trust and open communication that will extend beyond the preteen years and into adulthood. The investment in these communication skills is a lifelong investment in the parent-child relationship. The payoff is a more connected, supportive, and understanding family dynamic. This fosters resilience in the preteen and establishes a solid foundation for healthy emotional and social development. It's not just about solving problems; it's about creating a space where your preteen feels seen, heard, and understood, even amidst the complexities of adolescence.

Setting healthy boundaries is crucial during the preteen years, a period marked by a growing desire for independence coupled with the continued need for parental guidance and structure. This stage requires a delicate balancing act: providing the support and security preteens still need while simultaneously fostering a sense of autonomy and responsibility. The goal isn't to control, but to guide them toward making safe and responsible choices, equipping them with the skills they'll need as they navigate the complexities of adolescence and beyond.

The foundation of healthy boundaries lies in clear, age-appropriate rules and expectations. These shouldn't be arbitrary dictates, but rather guidelines established through open communication and collaborative decision-making whenever possible. Involving your preteen in the process helps them feel respected and understood, increasing the likelihood of adherence. For example, instead of simply imposing a curfew, engage in a conversation about the reasons behind it – safety, sufficient sleep, and family time. Explain the consequences of violating the curfew and listen to their concerns or suggestions. This collaborative approach builds responsibility and fosters a sense of ownership over the rules.

Consistency, in enforcing consequences is equally important. Preteens thrive on predictability and clear understanding of cause and effect. If a rule is broken, the consequence should be applied fairly and consistently, without wavering. Inconsistency can breed confusion and undermine your authority. For example, if you've established a consequence for late-night phone use, ensure that this consequence is applied each time the rule is violated. This predictability helps preteens understand the expectations and the natural repercussions of their actions.

However, rigid adherence to rules without flexibility can be counterproductive. There needs to be room for exceptions and understanding. Life happens, and unforeseen circumstances can arise. Being willing to listen to your preteen's explanations and consider exceptional situations demonstrates empathy and builds trust. For example, if your preteen has a legitimate reason for missing curfew – a school event, a delayed bus – being willing to listen and adjust the rules accordingly shows you are reasonable and understanding, strengthening your relationship.

Another crucial aspect of setting boundaries is fostering a sense of responsibility and accountability. This involves giving preteens age-appropriate responsibilities and allowing them to experience the natural consequences of their choices. This could include assigning chores, managing their allowance, or being responsible for their belongings. The focus should be on guiding them through the process, providing support and guidance when needed, rather than taking over completely.

Let's explore some common areas where setting boundaries is particularly important:

Curfew: Setting a reasonable curfew is essential for ensuring your preteen's safety and well-being. The curfew should be discussed and agreed upon collaboratively, considering their age, maturity level, and activities. It's important to be flexible and adjust the curfew based on specific situations, such as school events or social gatherings. The consequences of violating the curfew should be clearly explained beforehand, fostering a sense of accountability.

Screen Time: Excessive screen time can negatively impact sleep, academic performance, and social skills. Setting limits on screen time is crucial, but it's important to engage in a conversation about the reasons behind these limits. Involve your preteen in creating a schedule that balances screen time with other activities, such as homework, physical activity, and family time. This fosters a sense of control and responsibility. The consequences for exceeding the agreed-upon screen time should be clearly defined and consistently enforced. It's also helpful to model healthy screen habits yourself.

Chores: Assigning age-appropriate chores helps preteens develop a sense of responsibility and contribution to the family. These chores should be clearly defined and age-appropriate, ensuring that they are not overwhelming or unrealistic. Regularly reviewing and adjusting the chore list ensures that the tasks remain relevant and appropriate to their developing capabilities. Providing positive reinforcement and acknowledging their contributions strengthens their sense of responsibility and builds their self-esteem.

Social Media and Online Activities: The digital world presents a unique set of challenges for preteens. Setting boundaries around social media usage is crucial to protect them from cyberbullying, online predators, and inappropriate content. This includes discussing responsible online behavior, establishing clear guidelines for online interactions, and monitoring their online activities. Open communication and regular conversations about their online experiences are vital, fostering a safe space to discuss concerns and seek guidance.

Handling violations of boundaries requires a sensitive and constructive approach. Instead of resorting to anger or punishment, engage in a calm and respectful conversation. Listen to your preteen's perspective, acknowledge their feelings, and work collaboratively to find a solution. Punishments should be focused on teaching responsibility and accountability, rather than simply inflicting pain. The goal is to guide them toward better decision-making skills and foster a sense of ownership over their actions.

It's important to remember that setting boundaries is an ongoing process, requiring adaptation and adjustment as your preteen grows and matures. Regular family meetings can provide a forum for discussing boundaries, reviewing expectations, and resolving conflicts. These meetings should be a safe space for open communication, where everyone feels comfortable expressing their needs and concerns. Flexibility and willingness to adapt boundaries are essential in navigating the complexities of the preteen years.

Ultimately, setting healthy boundaries is about fostering independence while ensuring safety and well-being. It's a delicate balance between providing structure and allowing for freedom of choice. By engaging in open communication, collaboratively establishing rules, and consistently enforcing consequences, parents can equip their preteens with the skills and understanding they need to make responsible decisions and thrive during this crucial developmental stage. The process is about guiding them towards self-regulation, resilience, and ultimately, becoming responsible, well-adjusted adults. Remember, this is not about control, but about nurturing growth, empowering choice, and building a strong, trusting parent-child relationship that will last a lifetime. The investment in setting clear and consistent boundaries pays off in immeasurable ways.

Creating a consistent and predictable environment through routines and rituals is a powerful tool for fostering open communication with preteens. These structured activities aren't merely about scheduling; they build a foundation of trust and shared experience, providing regular opportunities for connection and dialogue. Think of them as fertile ground where open communication can flourish. The key lies in making these routines meaningful and engaging, tailored to your family's unique dynamics and schedules.

Family dinners, often touted as a cornerstone of family connection, offer more than just sustenance. They present a daily opportunity for relaxed conversation, sharing of the day's events, and informal check-ins on each family member's emotional well-being. However, the success of family dinners relies on creating a positive and inclusive atmosphere. Avoid turning mealtimes into interrogation sessions or platforms for lectures. Instead, focus on engaging conversation, active listening, and genuine interest in your preteen's experiences. A simple, "How was your day?" can open the door to meaningful dialogue. You can also initiate conversations about current events, shared interests, or even funny anecdotes from your own day. Remember, the goal is to create a sense of community and shared experience, where everyone feels comfortable contributing. If your schedule makes daily dinners impossible, even a few times a week can make a difference. The consistency is key; your preteen will come to anticipate this dedicated family time and look forward to the connection it provides.

Beyond the dinner table, consider incorporating regular family game nights into your routine. Games offer a fun and lighthearted way to connect, reducing the pressure associated with more formal conversations. Board games, card games, or even video games (depending on your family's preferences) provide opportunities for friendly competition, laughter, and teamwork. They allow for spontaneous interaction and the emergence of natural conversations. The focus isn't necessarily on winning, but on engaging together, fostering camaraderie, and enjoying each other's company. Choose games that suit everyone's age and interests to ensure participation and enjoyment. Observing your preteen's interactions during these activities can offer valuable insights into their personality, social skills, and emotional state.

For families with busy schedules, incorporating short daily check-ins can be surprisingly effective. These don't have to be lengthy conversations; a few minutes before bed, or during a car ride, can provide sufficient time for a brief connection. Ask about their highlights and challenges of the day, their feelings about upcoming events, or simply share a funny moment from your day. These brief interactions demonstrate that you are attentive and present, showing that their experiences are important to you. These small gestures build emotional security and let your preteen know that you are readily available and willing to listen. Even a simple, "I love you" before bed can reaffirm your bond and leave a lasting positive impact.

Creating a consistent bedtime routine can also play a vital role in encouraging open communication. This routine should be calming and predictable, ideally involving activities like reading together, listening to calming music, or having a quiet conversation. This dedicated time before sleep provides an opportunity to reconnect after a busy day and facilitate a more relaxed conversation. Your preteen may be more willing to open up in a quieter, less pressured environment. This could be a perfect time to ask about their anxieties or concerns in a more gentle manner. Remember to avoid overwhelming them with complex questions or topics close to bedtime. Focus on creating a calming, positive atmosphere that encourages shared experiences and feelings of comfort.

Family rituals, even small ones, can greatly enhance communication and bonding. These could be anything from watching a specific movie together every Friday night to baking cookies together on weekends or having a weekly family hike. The key is that these activities become traditions, a consistent source of shared experience and connection. These shared moments create lasting memories and a sense of belonging, strengthening the emotional bonds within the family. They provide a platform for casual conversations and a relaxed atmosphere for sharing feelings and experiences, further cementing your communication.

But what if your preteen seems resistant to these efforts? Sometimes, the struggle isn't a lack of desire to connect but a difficulty in expressing themselves. Preteens often experience a wide range of emotions—anxiety about school, peer pressure, body image issues—that may be challenging to articulate. Remember, pushing for immediate openness can be counterproductive. Instead, approach these situations with empathy and patience. Let them know you are there for them, regardless of whether they feel comfortable sharing their feelings. Your consistent presence and unconditional love create a safe haven, a space where they can gradually feel comfortable opening up.

Creating a "worry box" or journal could offer a nonverbal avenue for communication. This can allow your preteen to write down their thoughts and feelings, which can be far easier than verbalizing them. You can read their entries together at their pace and comfort level, or they can choose to keep the journal private. Remember to emphasize that you are not there to judge but simply to listen and support them. You can even share your own worries and anxieties, demonstrating vulnerability and creating a more equal exchange.

Involving your preteen in creating and maintaining these routines and rituals can significantly enhance their participation and investment. Allow them to voice their preferences, contribute ideas, and even help decide on the specific activities. Their involvement will foster a sense of ownership and increase the likelihood of their engagement. This sense of autonomy and control can also be very empowering for a preteen navigating the challenging developmental phase of their lives. This can pave the way for open dialogue about their needs and expectations.

Remember, the goal isn't to create a perfect, meticulously planned schedule, but rather to establish a framework for consistent connection and open communication. Flexibility and adaptability are crucial, especially given the ever-changing dynamics of a preteen's life. Life inevitably throws curveballs; it's important to adjust routines as necessary, acknowledging that things don't always go as planned and being flexible will prevent frustration. The essential aspect is maintaining the core principle: dedicated time for connecting and engaging with your preteen. Even small adjustments demonstrate your willingness to meet them halfway, fostering understanding and empathy in the process.

Creating a positive environment where your preteen feels safe, seen, and understood takes consistent effort and genuine engagement. It's about more than just scheduling; it's about cultivating a loving, supportive, and open relationship, creating a strong foundation for their future emotional well-being. The investment in building these routines and rituals will yield immeasurable rewards, fostering stronger familial bonds and equipping your preteen with the essential communication skills they need to navigate the complexities of adolescence and beyond. The journey may have its bumps, but the destination—a strong, communicative, and loving relationship with your preteen—is well worth the effort. Remember, it's a journey of mutual understanding and growth, and embracing this journey together will strengthen your bond. Building these routines and rituals is not just about improving communication; it's about building a stronger, more resilient, and loving family unit.

Chapter 2
Navigating Academic Pressures

The transition to preteen years often marks a significant shift in academic demands. The once manageable workload transforms into a more complex landscape of assignments, tests, and projects, often accompanied by a heightened sense of competition and self-evaluation. This increased pressure can manifest in various ways, impacting not only a preteen's academic performance but also their overall well-being and communication with family. Understanding these pressures and their impact is the first step toward offering effective support and fostering open communication.

One common manifestation of academic stress is difficulty concentrating. A preteen who previously excelled in school might suddenly struggle to focus on their studies, exhibiting signs of inattention, daydreaming, or easily getting distracted. This lack of focus isn't necessarily a sign of laziness or defiance, but rather a symptom of underlying stress or anxiety. The sheer volume of academic tasks, combined with the social and emotional changes of adolescence, can overwhelm a preteen's ability to concentrate effectively. They might feel overwhelmed by the sheer amount of homework or find it difficult to manage their time effectively, leading to feelings of frustration and a sense of being constantly behind. This can then create a vicious cycle: the more behind they feel, the harder it becomes to focus, further exacerbating the problem.

Test anxiety is another significant challenge faced by many preteens. The pressure to perform well on tests can lead to significant stress, manifesting in physical symptoms like nausea, headaches, or difficulty sleeping. This anxiety can significantly impair a preteen's ability to recall information and perform to their full potential, even if they have a strong understanding of the material. The fear of failure, the weight of expectations, both self-imposed and external, can create an overwhelming sense of pressure that paralyzes their ability to function effectively during testing situations. This anxiety doesn't simply disappear once the test is over; it can linger, affecting their confidence and motivation for future academic endeavors.

Beyond concentration issues and test anxiety, feelings of inadequacy and low self-esteem can significantly impact a preteen's academic experience. Comparing themselves to peers, particularly in a competitive academic environment, can lead to negative self-perception. They may feel like they aren't "smart enough," "good enough," or "fast enough," leading to feelings of frustration and discouragement. Social media and its curated portrayals of success can further exacerbate these feelings, contributing to a constant pressure to conform to unrealistic standards. The constant comparison with seemingly perfect peers can significantly erode self-confidence and motivation to study, leading to a downward spiral of negative self-perception and academic underperformance.

Recognizing these signs of academic stress is crucial for parents. It's essential to differentiate between genuine academic struggles and simply adolescent behaviors. While some reluctance to study might be a phase, persistent difficulty concentrating, significant anxiety around tests, and consistent feelings of inadequacy often indicate underlying academic stress that requires attention and support. Open communication is essential; creating a safe space where your preteen feels comfortable sharing their struggles, without fear of judgment or punishment, is paramount. This might involve actively listening, validating their feelings, and offering reassurance and encouragement. Avoid dismissing their concerns or minimizing their anxieties; instead, approach their experiences with empathy and understanding.

However, offering support doesn't necessarily equate to taking over their academic responsibilities. While assisting with organization or study techniques can be helpful, it's vital to avoid micromanaging their work or becoming overly involved in their studies. The goal is to empower them to take ownership of their learning and develop effective coping mechanisms, not to shield them from academic challenges. This means guiding them, rather than doing their work for them. It's a delicate balance between providing support and fostering independence.

Creating a supportive, non-judgmental learning environment at home is vital. This involves establishing a dedicated study space, free from distractions, where they can focus on their work. It also means providing them with the necessary resources, such as appropriate study materials and quiet time. Ensuring adequate sleep, a healthy diet, and regular physical activity are also essential in supporting their academic performance and managing stress levels. These are all important factors that often get overlooked yet directly impact a preteen's ability to focus, learn and retain information.

Furthermore, fostering open communication about academic challenges is paramount. Regular check-ins about their schoolwork, not in the form of interrogations, but casual conversations, can help parents stay informed about their progress and any emerging challenges. This should be a two-way street; parents should also share their own experiences with challenges and successes, demonstrating that setbacks are a normal part of life and that overcoming them is a process of learning and growth. Sharing personal anecdotes can normalize struggles and show that everyone faces difficulties at times.

Encouraging a growth mindset, rather than a fixed mindset, is essential. A growth mindset emphasizes the belief that abilities and intelligence can be developed through effort and learning, whereas a fixed mindset believes these qualities are innate and unchangeable. Helping your preteen understand that mistakes are opportunities for learning and that persistent effort leads to improvement can significantly impact their resilience and motivation. This can involve focusing on their effort and progress rather than solely on grades or test scores. Celebrating small victories and acknowledging their efforts, regardless of the outcome, helps build confidence and perseverance.

Collaboration with their school is also crucial. Regular communication with teachers can provide valuable insights into your preteen's academic performance and challenges. This collaboration can lead to the development of individualized strategies to support their learning and address specific areas of concern. Open communication with educators can also help parents understand the overall academic expectations and pressures their child faces, providing a broader context for understanding their behavior and emotional state.

In cases where academic stress becomes overwhelming or significantly impacts their well-being, seeking professional help is essential. A child psychologist or therapist can provide tailored support and coping strategies to help your preteen manage their anxiety, improve their study skills, and develop healthy coping mechanisms. Early intervention can prevent the development of more severe problems and significantly improve their academic and emotional well-being. This professional support can complement the efforts of parents and educators, creating a holistic approach to addressing academic pressures and promoting the child's overall well-being.

Ultimately, navigating the academic pressures of the preteen years requires a collaborative effort between parents, educators, and, most importantly, the preteen themselves. By fostering open communication, creating a supportive learning environment, and emphasizing a growth mindset, parents can equip their preteens with the resilience and skills they need to navigate the challenges of adolescence and achieve their academic potential. Remember, the goal isn't just about achieving high grades, but about fostering a healthy relationship with learning and cultivating a lifelong love for education. Supporting your preteen through these challenges builds their confidence, teaches them valuable life skills, and strengthens the bond between parent and child. This support is not just about academics; it's about nurturing their emotional well-being and setting them up for success in all aspects of their lives.

Effective communication is the cornerstone of successfully navigating the academic landscape with your preteen. While fostering a supportive home environment and cultivating a growth mindset are crucial, equally important is the ability to communicate effectively with teachers and school officials. This collaboration is not merely beneficial; it's essential for ensuring your child receives the appropriate support and understanding they need to thrive academically. Building strong relationships with your child's teachers and school administrators is an investment in their future success.

Establishing open communication with teachers starts long before any problems arise. Attend parent-teacher conferences, even if your child seems to be doing well. This proactive approach allows you to get to know the teacher, understand their teaching style and expectations, and build rapport. It also provides an opportunity to discuss your child's strengths and weaknesses, setting the stage for future collaborations. Don't wait for a crisis to reach out; regular communication prevents minor issues from escalating into major problems.

When communicating with teachers, adopt a respectful and collaborative tone. Avoid accusatory language or placing blame. Frame your concerns as a shared objective: "I'm concerned about [child's name]'s recent drop in grades, and I was hoping we could collaborate on finding strategies to help them improve." This approach fosters a partnership, inviting the teacher to work alongside you rather than feeling confronted or defensive. Remember, teachers want what's best for your child; they are your allies in this process.

Focus on observable behaviors and specific examples. Instead of saying "My child isn't doing well in math," try "I've noticed [child's name] has struggled with completing homework assignments in the past two weeks, and their recent test scores show a significant decline." This provides the teacher with concrete information that is easier to address and investigate. Vague complaints are less effective than clear, detailed descriptions of the issue.

Listen actively to the teacher's perspective. They may have insights into your child's behavior or academic performance that you haven't considered. Ask clarifying questions to ensure you understand their observations and any strategies they've already implemented. This active listening demonstrates respect and allows for a more comprehensive understanding of the situation. Resist the urge to interrupt; instead, allow the teacher to fully articulate their viewpoint before responding.

Discuss potential solutions collaboratively. Instead of simply stating your preferred course of action, brainstorm solutions together. This could include adjustments to homework routines, additional tutoring, or alternative teaching methods. By working together, you and the teacher can create a tailored plan that addresses your child's specific needs and learning style. This collaborative approach ensures that everyone feels involved and invested in the success of the plan.

Document all communication, both written and verbal. Keep copies of emails, notes from meetings, and any other relevant documentation. This provides a clear record of the communication history, which can be invaluable if further intervention is needed. It also helps ensure that everyone is on the same page regarding the agreed-upon strategies and the timeline for implementing them.

Be patient and persistent. Addressing academic issues often requires time and effort. Don't get discouraged if you don't see immediate results. Regularly check in with the teacher to monitor progress and make adjustments to the plan as needed. Persistence is crucial in ensuring that your child receives the support they need to overcome their academic challenges.

Beyond teachers, communication with school counselors and administrators is also crucial, especially if you are facing more significant challenges or systemic issues. School counselors can provide valuable insights into your child's social and emotional well-being, which often intertwine with their academic performance. They can also connect you with additional resources and support services available within the school.

When communicating with administrators, be clear and concise, providing a detailed explanation of the situation and what you are hoping to achieve. Be prepared to provide documentation to support your claims. Maintain a professional demeanor throughout the communication process, even if you are feeling frustrated or angry. Remember that administrators are there to support both students and parents; approaching them with a collaborative spirit will generally yield better results.

If your child has a diagnosed learning disability or other special needs, open communication with the special education team is essential. This team includes special education teachers, case managers, and potentially other professionals such as therapists or psychologists. Work closely with them to develop an Individualized Education Program (IEP) or a 504 plan, which outlines the specific accommodations and support services your child needs to succeed in school. Regular meetings and consistent communication are crucial to ensure that the IEP or 504 plan remains effective and meets your child's evolving needs.

Remember that conflict can sometimes arise, and it is important to approach disagreements constructively. If conflict does arise, focus on finding common ground and solutions. Avoid making personal attacks or engaging in unproductive arguments. Seek to understand the other person's perspective before stating your own. If a resolution cannot be reached through direct communication, consider involving a mediator or seeking guidance from the school administration. The goal is always to advocate for your child's best interests in a respectful and productive manner.

In addition to formal communication, consider informal strategies to enhance your communication with the school. Volunteer in your child's classroom or participate in school events. This provides valuable opportunities to interact with teachers and other parents, fostering a sense of community and strengthening relationships. Informal interactions can provide a more relaxed setting for casual conversations about your child's progress and any concerns you might have.

Ultimately, effective communication with the school is a crucial component of supporting your preteen's academic success. By building strong relationships with educators and administrators, engaging in proactive and respectful communication, and collaboratively addressing challenges, you can create a supportive environment that enables your child to thrive both academically and emotionally. Remember that this partnership is essential; it's not a battle but a collaborative effort to help your child reach their full potential. This collaborative approach creates a foundation for mutual understanding and successful navigation of the academic journey. Your involvement is a significant investment in your child's future and their relationship with learning.

Shifting the focus from solely grades to a broader appreciation for learning is paramount. While good grades are a reflection of effort and understanding, they shouldn't be the sole measure of a child's academic success or their self-worth. Instead, cultivate a growth mindset—the belief that intelligence and abilities are not fixed but can be developed through dedication and effort. This empowers children to embrace challenges, view mistakes as learning opportunities, and persevere in the face of setbacks.

Encourage your preteen to view setbacks not as failures, but as valuable learning experiences. Help them analyze what went wrong, identify areas for improvement, and develop strategies to overcome obstacles. This approach fosters resilience and a positive attitude toward challenges. Frame academic struggles as opportunities for growth and development, highlighting the process of learning rather than solely focusing on the outcome. Instead of dwelling on a poor grade, ask questions like, "What did you learn from this experience?", "What strategies can we use to approach this differently next time?", and "What resources might be helpful?" This shift in perspective encourages them to actively participate in their own learning journey.

Intrinsic motivation, the drive to learn for the sheer pleasure of it, is far more sustainable than extrinsic motivation, which relies on external rewards like grades or praise. To foster intrinsic motivation, connect learning to your child's interests. If they're passionate about art, incorporate art-related projects into their studies. If they love animals, explore science projects related to zoology or conservation. This personalized approach makes learning more engaging and enjoyable, boosting their intrinsic motivation.

Cultivate curiosity and a thirst for knowledge by providing enriching experiences outside of the traditional school curriculum. Trips to museums, science centers, historical sites, and libraries offer hands-on learning opportunities that spark interest and foster a love of discovery. Encourage reading for pleasure, not just for school assignments. Visit bookstores, libraries, and let them choose books that capture their imagination. Discussions about the books they read, fostering critical thinking and expanding their understanding of the world.

Embrace self-directed learning. Allow your child to explore topics that genuinely interest them, even if they are not directly related to their school curriculum. This fosters a sense of ownership and autonomy over their learning, making it more meaningful and engaging. Encourage them to pursue hobbies, join clubs, or participate in activities that challenge them and broaden their horizons. This can range from coding clubs to sports teams to volunteering, all offering opportunities for skill development and self-discovery.

Provide opportunities for creative expression. Encourage your preteen to explore different artistic mediums, whether it's painting, drawing, writing, music, or drama. Creative pursuits foster problem-solving skills, critical thinking, and self-expression, all vital components of a well-rounded education. Even seemingly unrelated creative activities can enhance cognitive abilities that are transferable to academic pursuits. For example, playing a musical instrument can improve memory and coordination skills, while writing stories enhances vocabulary and communication.

Encourage collaboration and teamwork. Group projects, study sessions with peers, and collaborative games all provide opportunities for your child to learn from others, develop social skills, and appreciate diverse perspectives. These collaborative experiences can make learning more engaging and help your child develop a sense of community and belonging. It's not just about individual achievement, but also the power of shared effort and mutual support.

Incorporate technology thoughtfully. While technology can be a distraction, it can also be a powerful tool for learning. Explore educational apps, online courses, and interactive learning platforms that cater to your child's interests and learning style. However, ensure that technology use is balanced and purposeful, avoiding excessive screen time and focusing on enriching digital experiences.

Celebrate effort and progress, not just results. Acknowledge and praise your child's efforts, persistence, and improvements, regardless of their grades. This reinforces the importance of hard work and dedication, fostering a growth mindset. Focus on celebrating milestones and progress rather than solely focusing on achieving perfection. This encouragement helps them build self-confidence and develop resilience in the face of challenges.

Foster a positive and supportive home learning environment. Create a designated space for homework and studying that is free from distractions. Provide necessary resources, such as books, stationery, and technology, and ensure that your child has a comfortable and well-lit workspace. This dedicated space promotes focus and productivity, creating a positive association with learning.

Engage in regular conversations about school. Ask your child about their day, what they learned, and what they found challenging or enjoyable. Listen actively and show genuine interest in their experiences. These conversations provide valuable insights into their learning process and allow you to address any concerns proactively. These open discussions create a supportive and safe space where your preteen feels comfortable sharing their thoughts and feelings.

Model a love of learning. Show your child that learning is a lifelong journey, not just something confined to school. Share your own interests and passions, and demonstrate a willingness to learn new things. This modeling behaviour is a powerful influence on your child's attitude toward learning. It teaches them that learning is not just an academic pursuit but an integral part of life, fostering continuous growth and development.

Seek professional support when needed. If you are concerned about your child's academic performance or emotional well-being, don't hesitate to seek professional help. A psychologist, educational specialist, or school counselor can provide valuable insights and support. Early intervention can make a significant difference in addressing any underlying issues and helping your child thrive academically and emotionally. Remember that seeking professional help is a sign of strength and responsibility, not weakness or failure.

Remember that fostering a positive attitude towards learning is a long-term process that requires patience, consistency, and a collaborative approach. By focusing on intrinsic motivation, self-directed learning, and a growth mindset, you can help your preteen develop a lifelong love of learning, which will serve them well throughout their lives. It's not just about grades; it's about developing a passion for knowledge, critical thinking, and a lifelong journey of discovery. This approach creates a foundation for academic success and overall personal fulfillment. Your efforts in cultivating this positive attitude towards learning will empower your child to embrace challenges, overcome setbacks, and ultimately reach their full potential. This positive and holistic approach transforms learning from a chore into an engaging and fulfilling experience.

Furthermore, consider incorporating real-world applications of learned concepts to reinforce learning and demonstrate its practical value. For instance, if your child is learning about fractions in math, connect this to baking or cooking, allowing them to measure ingredients and experience the practical application of fractions. If they are learning about history, visit historical sites or museums to bring the subject to life. This hands-on approach makes learning more relevant and engaging, demonstrating the practical value of their studies.

Encourage self-reflection and goal setting. Help your child identify their strengths and weaknesses, set realistic goals, and develop strategies for achieving them. Regularly review progress and adjust goals as needed. This process fosters self-awareness, responsibility, and a sense of ownership over their learning journey. Regular self-reflection also allows them to understand their learning styles and preferences, leading to more effective learning strategies.

Finally, remember to create a supportive and encouraging environment where mistakes are seen as opportunities for growth. Avoid criticism and focus on providing constructive feedback and encouragement. Celebrate small victories and acknowledge their efforts, fostering a positive learning experience. This positive and supportive approach cultivates self-confidence and resilience, enabling your preteen to navigate academic challenges with a positive attitude and a growth mindset. This nurturing environment fosters a love of learning that extends beyond the classroom.

The preteen years are a whirlwind of growth, discovery, and burgeoning independence. Academic pressures are mounting, and alongside schoolwork comes the desire to explore extracurricular activities, social engagements, and personal interests. Finding the right balance is crucial for both academic success and the healthy development of your child. This delicate dance requires open communication, collaborative planning, and a willingness to adapt as your child's needs and interests evolve. The key isn't about restricting activities; it's about empowering your child to manage their time effectively and make conscious choices about their priorities.

Begin by fostering open and honest conversations about your child's commitments. Don't assume you know their schedule or their capacity. Actively listen to their perspectives on the demands of school, their extracurricular involvement, and their personal time. Ask open-ended questions such as, "What are you finding challenging about your schedule right now?", "Which activities are you most passionate about?", and "How do you feel about the balance between your schoolwork and your extracurriculars?" These conversations create a safe space for your child to express their concerns, frustrations, and priorities without feeling judged or pressured.

From these conversations, you can collaboratively develop strategies for managing time more effectively. This isn't about imposing a rigid schedule, but about empowering your child to take ownership of their time. Involve them in the planning process. Together, create a visual schedule— perhaps a whiteboard or a shared digital calendar—that outlines schoolwork, extracurricular activities, social events, and personal time. This visual representation provides clarity and helps your child track their commitments, promoting a sense of organization and control.

Time management skills are not innate; they are learned and refined over time. Introduce your child to various time management techniques, such as prioritization matrices, time blocking, and the Pomodoro Technique. Explore which strategies resonate best with your child's learning style and personality. Avoid overwhelming them with too many techniques at once. Instead, introduce one at a time and allow them ample opportunity to practice and master it before moving on to the next. Patience and encouragement are key.

Prioritization is a fundamental aspect of time management. Help your child distinguish between high-priority tasks (those that are crucial for academic success) and lower-priority tasks. This might involve identifying core subjects that require more attention or assignments with approaching deadlines. Encourage them to tackle high-priority tasks first, creating a sense of accomplishment and reducing stress associated with looming deadlines.

The concept of "productive procrastination" can be a valuable tool. This doesn't mean delaying important tasks; it means utilizing shorter breaks or downtime between tasks for more efficient work. Instead of watching television, suggest a short walk or a quick game to refocus and re-energize before tackling the next assignment. This balanced approach helps maintain focus and prevents burnout.

Alongside time management, instill the importance of setting realistic goals and expectations. It's crucial to avoid overcommitment and encourage your child to say "no" to activities they don't genuinely enjoy or that would overwhelm their schedule. This is a critical life skill that fosters self-awareness and a sense of agency over their time. Teach them to assess their capacity, recognize their limitations, and prioritize activities that truly matter.

Seek opportunities to integrate their extracurricular interests with their academic pursuits. For instance, if your child is passionate about music, explore the connection between music theory and mathematics. If they are involved in sports, encourage them to analyze statistics and improve their performance through data-driven strategies. This integration demonstrates the relevance of academics to their passions, creating a sense of purpose and motivation.

Celebrate their successes, no matter how small. Acknowledge their efforts in balancing their commitments, and focus on their progress rather than solely on the outcome. This positive reinforcement fosters resilience and self-esteem, empowering them to persevere in the face of challenges. Encourage self-reflection by having them periodically review their schedules and assess the effectiveness of their time management strategies.

Remember that finding the perfect balance is an ongoing process, not a destination. Regularly revisit your child's schedule and make adjustments as needed. Be flexible and understanding; life happens, and unexpected events can disrupt the best-laid plans. The ability to adapt and adjust is as important as the initial planning.

Collaborate with the school to understand their expectations and workload. Teachers can provide insights into the demands of specific courses and potential areas of support. Open communication with the school can help you create a schedule that aligns with academic requirements and reduces unnecessary stress.

Engage in regular check-ins with your child to monitor their workload, identify any potential challenges, and ensure they have the support they need. These conversations create opportunities for early intervention, preventing smaller problems from escalating into major stressors. Focus on open-ended questions to understand your child's perspective.

Consider seeking professional help if your child is consistently struggling with stress management, time management, or academic performance. A therapist or counselor can provide tools and strategies for coping with stress and improving organizational skills. They can also help identify and address any underlying emotional or behavioral issues that may be contributing to the challenges.

Ultimately, the goal is not to create a perfectly balanced schedule, but to empower your child to develop the skills and strategies to navigate the complexities of academic demands, extracurricular activities, and personal commitments. By fostering open communication, promoting collaborative planning, and emphasizing time management skills, you can help your child thrive during these formative years, developing a strong sense of self-efficacy and a healthy approach to life's many demands. This process nurtures not only their academic success, but also their emotional well-being and overall personal development, fostering resilience and a positive approach to life's challenges. It's about equipping them with lifelong skills, empowering them to make conscious choices, and celebrating their individual strengths. This holistic approach ensures that your preteen experiences a supportive environment conducive to both academic excellence and overall personal growth. The journey itself is an education, teaching your child valuable life skills for future success.

Remember, this is not a one-size-fits-all solution. Each child is unique, with their own individual strengths, weaknesses, and learning styles. What works for one preteen may not work for another. The key is to be flexible, adapt your approach as needed, and above all, maintain open communication and a collaborative relationship with your child throughout this crucial developmental stage. The goal is to build confidence and resilience, helping them to navigate the challenges and enjoy the rewards of their efforts. This nurturing process will empower them not just for their preteen years but for the challenges and opportunities that lie ahead in their lives. Supporting their balanced development creates a strong foundation for success in all aspects of their life. By understanding their needs and offering tailored support, you equip them for the future, fostering independence and self-reliance.

Finally, consider involving your child in activities that promote mindfulness and stress reduction. Yoga, meditation, or even regular physical activity can be beneficial in managing stress and improving focus. These practices can be incorporated into their daily routine, providing a healthy outlet for managing the pressures of academics and extracurricular activities. Encourage a balanced lifestyle that incorporates both intellectual pursuits and healthy lifestyle choices. This holistic approach promotes well-being and helps your preteen navigate the challenges of this developmental stage with greater ease and resilience. The focus should be on creating a positive and supportive environment where your child feels empowered to succeed, not just academically but in all aspects of their life.

The journey of raising a preteen is already complex, navigating the balance between academic pressures, social life, and personal growth. This complexity intensifies significantly when your child has a learning disability or special needs. Understanding and addressing these challenges requires a multifaceted approach that combines effective communication, advocacy, and a deep understanding of your child's unique learning style. This necessitates a strong partnership between parents, educators, and any other professionals involved in your child's care.

Open and honest communication forms the cornerstone of this partnership. This means actively listening to your child, understanding their perspectives on their learning challenges, and validating their feelings. Often, preteens with learning disabilities feel frustrated, overwhelmed, or even ashamed of their difficulties. Creating a safe and supportive space for them to express these feelings without judgment is crucial for their self-esteem and willingness to engage in the necessary support systems. Ask open-ended questions like, "What parts of school are you finding most difficult?", "How does this make you feel?", and "What do you think would help you feel more successful?".

Their answers will provide invaluable insights into their experiences and help you tailor your support accordingly.

This open communication extends beyond your child to encompass educators, therapists, and other professionals involved in their education and well-being. Regular meetings with teachers are essential to understand your child's academic progress, identify any areas where they are struggling, and collaboratively develop strategies for success. These meetings should not be confrontational, but rather collaborative discussions aimed at finding solutions. Prepare beforehand by jotting down your observations, concerns, and questions. Come prepared with specific examples of your child's challenges and successes. This focused approach will allow for productive discussions and a collaborative approach to problem-solving.

Similarly, maintain open communication with therapists, psychologists, or other specialists who may be involved in your child's care. These professionals can provide valuable insights into your child's learning style, emotional well-being, and potential strategies to support their academic and social-emotional development. Regular updates between parents and these professionals are crucial to ensure a coordinated and effective support system. Share observations from home, highlighting your child's strengths and challenges in different settings. This collaborative approach ensures consistent support across all aspects of your child's life.

Understanding your child's specific learning disability or special need is fundamental. This requires actively seeking information from educators, therapists, and researching available resources. Depending on the specific diagnosis, your child may require accommodations in the classroom, such as extended time on tests, preferential seating, or the use of assistive technology. Familiarize yourself with the Individuals with Disabilities Education Act (IDEA) or equivalent legislation in your country to understand your rights and the support services available to your child. This knowledge empowers you to advocate effectively for your child's needs within the educational system.

Advocating for your child's needs goes beyond simply attending meetings and communicating with professionals. It involves actively participating in the development of your child's Individualized Education Program (IEP) or 504 plan, if applicable. Understand the goals, objectives, and strategies outlined in these documents and ensure they align with your child's needs and abilities. Don't hesitate to ask clarifying questions or propose modifications to better support your child's learning. Remember, you are your child's strongest advocate, and your active involvement is crucial in ensuring they receive the appropriate support and resources.

Beyond formal educational settings, supporting your child's unique learning style at home is equally important. This may involve adapting your parenting strategies to accommodate their specific needs. For instance, if your child has difficulty with reading comprehension, try using audiobooks or graphic novels. If they struggle with organization, create visual schedules or checklists to help them manage their tasks. Find creative ways to engage them in learning, utilizing their interests and strengths to make the learning process more enjoyable and accessible. This approach encourages a positive attitude towards learning and helps build their confidence.

Celebrate your child's successes, no matter how small. Focus on their progress and efforts, rather than solely on their grades or achievements. Positive reinforcement fosters self-esteem and motivates them to continue striving towards their goals. Acknowledge their perseverance and resilience in facing challenges. This supportive environment builds confidence and reduces feelings of frustration or inadequacy.

Building their self-advocacy skills is crucial for their long-term success. Encourage them to communicate their needs to teachers and other adults. Role-play scenarios to help them practice expressing their needs and asking for support. This empowers them to take ownership of their learning and develop a sense of agency over their educational experience. This will be a valuable life skill that will benefit them far beyond their preteen years.

Remember that seeking support is a sign of strength, not weakness. Don't hesitate to reach out to support groups, online communities, or other parents who have children with similar learning disabilities or special needs. Sharing experiences, exchanging strategies, and receiving emotional support can be invaluable in navigating the challenges of parenting a child with special needs. These connections can create a sense of community and shared understanding, which helps to alleviate feelings of isolation and provides a wealth of practical advice and emotional support.

Navigating the academic pressures faced by preteens with learning disabilities or special needs requires patience, persistence, and a deep commitment to understanding and supporting your child's individual learning style. By fostering open communication with your child, educators, and other professionals; by becoming an active advocate for your child's needs; and by creating a supportive and understanding home environment, you can empower your child to achieve their full potential and develop a positive and confident approach to learning. This requires a holistic approach that focuses not only on academics but also on their emotional well-being and social development. Remember that celebrating their strengths and focusing on progress, rather than solely outcomes, builds resilience and self-confidence. Your unwavering support and understanding are the most valuable tools in your child's journey to success. The investment in time and effort will not only benefit your child academically but will also nurture their overall personal growth and empower them to become self-reliant and successful individuals. The journey might be demanding, but it is undoubtedly rewarding as you witness your child overcome challenges and flourish.

Chapter 3
Navigating Peer Influence and Social Dynamics

T he preteen years mark a significant shift in a child's social landscape. While family remains a cornerstone of their lives, the influence of peers exponentially increases, shaping their self-perception, values, and behaviors in profound ways. Understanding the importance of peer relationships during this critical developmental stage is paramount for parents seeking to guide their children successfully through preadolescence. This isn't simply about friendships; it's about the complex interplay of social dynamics, group dynamics, and the evolving sense of self within a peer context.

Peer relationships serve as a crucial testing ground for developing social skills. Preteens navigate intricate social hierarchies, learning to negotiate conflicts, cooperate, compromise, and build empathy through interactions with their peers. These experiences, while sometimes challenging, are essential for acquiring the social intelligence necessary for navigating future relationships, both personal and professional. Success in these interactions builds confidence and self-efficacy, fostering a sense of competence and belonging. Conversely, negative experiences can impact self-esteem and social confidence, leading to social isolation or withdrawal.

The influence of peer groups extends beyond the acquisition of social skills; it plays a vital role in the development of self-esteem and identity. Preteens often look to their peer groups for validation and acceptance, seeking to fit in and belong. This desire for belonging can be a powerful motivator, influencing their choices, behaviors, and even their self-perception. Positive peer groups offer support, encouragement, and a sense of community, strengthening self-esteem and promoting a positive self-image. Conversely, negative peer groups can exert considerable pressure, leading to risky behaviors, low self-esteem, and a distorted sense of self.

Identity formation during preadolescence is deeply intertwined with peer relationships. Preteens experiment with different roles and identities within their peer groups, trying on different personas and observing the reactions of their peers. This process of social experimentation is crucial for developing a sense of self and understanding their place in the world. The feedback received from their peers shapes their understanding of themselves and influences their self-perception. This process is particularly important for preteens who might be exploring their sexuality, gender identity, or other aspects of their personality. The support or rejection they receive from their peers can significantly affect their emotional well-being and the path they take in their identity development. A supportive peer group can offer a safe space for exploration and experimentation, while a negative or rejecting group can cause significant distress and confusion.

Parental support and guidance are crucial in navigating the complexities of peer relationships during preadolescence. Parents shouldn't aim to control their child's friendships but should instead focus on providing support, guidance, and a framework for healthy social interaction. This starts with open communication and active listening. Create an environment where your preteen feels comfortable sharing their experiences with their peers, both positive and negative. Ask open-ended questions to understand their perspectives and encourage them to reflect on their social interactions. For example, asking "How did that interaction make you feel?" or "What could you have done differently?" can encourage critical self-reflection.

Parental guidance should extend to helping preteens develop healthy coping mechanisms for dealing with peer pressure and conflict. This involves teaching them assertiveness skills, conflict resolution strategies, and the importance of setting boundaries. Role-playing scenarios can be beneficial in helping them practice these skills in a safe environment. The goal isn't to eliminate conflict, but to equip them with the tools to navigate it effectively and develop resilience. Parents can also model healthy conflict resolution and boundary-setting in their own relationships, providing a practical example for their children to emulate.

Another crucial aspect of parental guidance involves fostering a healthy balance between peer relationships and family relationships. While peer relationships become increasingly important during preadolescence, the family remains a vital source of support and security. Encourage family time and activities that strengthen family bonds. This reinforces the importance of the family unit even as your preteen increasingly seeks independence and connection with their peers. Make sure your preteen understands that you're there for them, offering a safe space to discuss problems or concerns related to their friendships or social interactions. This creates a secure base from which they can navigate the sometimes turbulent waters of peer relationships.

Furthermore, parents should remain actively involved in their child's social life, but without being overbearing. Knowing their friends, their activities, and their social circles can provide valuable insights into their social dynamics. This doesn't involve constant monitoring or surveillance, but a genuine interest in their social world, fostering a trusting relationship where they feel comfortable sharing information. This engagement allows for early detection of any potential problems or risky behaviors. It also enables you to proactively intervene, providing support and guidance when necessary.

It's important to remember that navigating peer influence doesn't involve dictating friendships or trying to control their social lives. Preteens need the freedom to develop their own relationships and friendships, learning from their experiences. However, parental guidance should focus on fostering healthy relationships and equipping them with the skills to navigate social complexities. The goal is to empower them to make healthy choices, manage conflict effectively, and develop strong and supportive peer relationships that contribute to their overall well-being.

Parents also need to be mindful of their own communication style and avoid unintentionally creating conflicts between family and peer relationships. Avoid making negative or dismissive remarks about their friends, even if you have concerns. This can damage trust and create a barrier to open communication. Instead, focus on expressing your concerns in a non-judgmental way, focusing on behaviors and potential consequences, rather than personal attacks on their friends or their character. This approach helps them understand your perspective without feeling defensive or alienated.

In cases where there are significant concerns about negative peer influence, such as involvement in risky behaviors or bullying, parental intervention is essential. This may involve talking to the child's friends, their parents, or even school authorities. The approach should be collaborative, focusing on finding solutions and fostering positive change. Early intervention is crucial in addressing such situations before they escalate into more serious problems. Seeking professional help from a child psychologist or therapist may be beneficial in complex cases. This approach provides a neutral third party perspective and specialized skills to help resolve conflicts and develop effective strategies.

The importance of peer relationships during preadolescence cannot be overstated. These relationships shape a child's social, emotional, and identity development. Parents play a crucial role in supporting their child's navigation of this complex social landscape, not by controlling their friendships, but by providing guidance, support, and the tools they need to build healthy and positive relationships. Open communication, proactive engagement, and a focus on fostering healthy coping mechanisms are essential elements of effective parenting during these critical years. The investment in time and effort will reap significant rewards, leading to a well-adjusted preteen with strong social skills, self-esteem, and a solid foundation for future success. Remember, the goal is to empower your preteen to build meaningful connections, learn from their experiences, and develop the social intelligence needed to thrive in the ever-evolving social world.

Addressing peer pressure effectively requires a multifaceted approach that goes beyond simply telling a preteen to "say no." It necessitates open communication, fostering critical thinking skills, and equipping them with the tools to navigate challenging social situations confidently. Begin by creating a safe space where your preteen feels comfortable sharing their experiences, both positive and negative, without fear of judgment or reprisal. Avoid dismissing their concerns or downplaying the significance of peer influence. Instead, validate their feelings and acknowledge the pressure they might be experiencing. This approach fosters trust and strengthens your relationship, making them more likely to seek your guidance in the future.

Open-ended questions are invaluable in understanding your preteen's perspective. Instead of asking leading questions like, "Did your friends pressure you to do that?", try asking, "Tell me about what happened with your friends today." or "How did that situation make you feel?". This encourages them to articulate their experiences and reflect on their emotions, fostering critical thinking and self-awareness. Active listening is paramount; pay attention not only to their words but also to their nonverbal cues, such as body language and tone of voice. This demonstrates genuine interest and reinforces their sense of being heard and understood.

One effective strategy is to role-play different scenarios involving peer pressure. This allows your preteen to practice assertive communication and boundary-setting skills in a safe environment. Present them with hypothetical situations, such as being offered alcohol or drugs, or being pressured to engage in risky behaviors. Work together to develop strategies for responding assertively, such as saying "no" clearly and directly, explaining their reasons, and suggesting alternative activities. Rehearsing these responses builds their confidence and equips them with the skills to handle similar situations in real life.

Teaching your preteen about the importance of self-esteem and healthy boundaries is crucial in resisting peer pressure. Help them understand that their self-worth is not contingent upon the approval of others. Encourage them to identify their values and prioritize their own well-being, even if it means disagreeing with their friends. This involves teaching them to recognize and reject manipulative tactics often used in peer pressure situations. For instance, if friends use guilt or shame to pressure them into something, they can learn to recognize this manipulation and stand their ground.

Conflict resolution skills are essential for navigating the complexities of peer relationships. Preteens will inevitably encounter disagreements and conflicts with their friends. Equip them with strategies for resolving conflicts constructively, emphasizing communication, compromise, and empathy. Encourage active listening, allowing each party to express their perspective without interruption. Help them to identify common ground and work together to find mutually acceptable solutions. Emphasize the importance of respecting differing viewpoints and seeking win-win solutions whenever possible. This teaches them valuable negotiation skills and prevents conflicts from escalating into larger issues.

Sometimes, peer conflict might stem from misunderstandings or misinterpretations. Teach your preteen the importance of clarifying communication to avoid unnecessary conflicts. Encourage them to ask clarifying questions to ensure they understand their friend's perspective. They should also be encouraged to express themselves clearly and directly, avoiding passive-aggressive behaviors or unclear communication that could lead to misunderstandings. This fosters stronger, more effective communication and prevents conflicts based on miscommunication.

However, some conflicts might require the intervention of adults. If conflicts become serious or involve bullying, violence, or other harmful behaviors, it's crucial for parents to get involved. This doesn't mean taking over the situation but providing guidance and support to help your preteen navigate the conflict constructively. Explain that it's acceptable to seek help from trusted adults, such as teachers, counselors, or other family members, when needed. This reinforces that they're not alone in dealing with conflicts and that seeking support is a sign of strength, not weakness.

Building healthy relationships requires mutual respect and understanding. Teach your preteen the importance of setting boundaries and respecting the boundaries of others. Explain that it's acceptable to say "no" to requests or activities that make them feel uncomfortable. They should also learn to respect the "no" of others, even if they disagree with it. This approach establishes a foundation of mutual respect and prevents conflicts stemming from boundary violations.

When addressing peer conflicts, the focus should be on finding solutions rather than assigning blame. This requires focusing on behaviors and consequences rather than making personal attacks. Help your preteen understand the impact of their actions and the actions of others. Teach them to take responsibility for their own actions while acknowledging the role of others in the conflict. This promotes constructive problem-solving and facilitates reconciliation.

Encourage your preteen to evaluate the nature of their friendships. While social pressures are significant during preadolescence, fostering a sense of discerning judgment is vital. Explain the importance of choosing friends who respect them, support their values, and encourage positive behavior. Explain that it's okay to distance themselves from friendships that are toxic or detrimental to their well-being. This empowers them to make informed decisions about their friendships and foster positive social circles.

Understanding social hierarchies and navigating group dynamics are equally essential. Preteens often find themselves in situations where they are compelled to conform to group norms or face social rejection. Educate them on the dynamics of peer groups and help them identify unhealthy group pressures. For instance, discuss the potential for negative influence in groups focused on risky behaviors, such as substance abuse or bullying. This awareness helps them to make informed decisions about their social interactions.

Furthermore, it is critical to foster a strong parent-child relationship built on trust and open communication. Create an environment where your preteen feels comfortable talking to you about their social lives and challenges. This requires active listening, empathy, and avoiding judgment. It also means showing genuine interest in their friendships and their social activities. This approach allows you to identify potential problems early on and address them before they escalate. Ensure they understand you're there to support them and guide them, not to control their lives.

Beyond direct conversations, involve your preteen in activities that strengthen their self-esteem and build resilience. Encourage participation in activities they enjoy, whether it's sports, arts, music, or community involvement. This helps build their confidence and provides a sense of belonging outside of their peer group. Positive experiences in other aspects of their lives can buffer the negative effects of peer pressure and foster a stronger sense of self.

Finally, remember that seeking professional help is not a sign of failure. If you're struggling to address peer pressure or conflict resolution issues with your preteen, consider consulting a child psychologist or therapist. These professionals offer specialized knowledge and tools to help families navigate these challenges effectively. They can provide guidance, support, and strategies tailored to your family's unique situation. Don't hesitate to seek help when needed; it's a sign of proactive and responsible parenting. Your preteen's well-being is paramount, and seeking expert guidance is a testament to your commitment to their healthy development.

Promoting positive peer relationships is a cornerstone of a preteen's healthy development. While navigating the complexities of social dynamics, it's crucial for parents to actively guide their children toward forming healthy friendships and developing robust social skills. This involves not only identifying unhealthy friendships but also proactively fostering positive interactions and equipping children with the tools to navigate social challenges successfully. This section offers a comprehensive guide to support parents in this vital role.

Recognizing the signs of unhealthy friendships is the first crucial step. An unhealthy friendship often involves consistent negativity, conflict, or manipulation. Look for patterns of constant arguing, betrayal, or situations where your preteen is consistently feeling unhappy or stressed after spending time with a particular friend. These friendships might involve pressure to engage in risky behaviors such as substance abuse, shoplifting, or bullying. The friend might exhibit controlling behavior, attempt to isolate your child from other friends and family, or consistently put your child down, undermining their self-esteem. A significant red flag is a dramatic shift in your child's behavior, including changes in mood, grades, or overall demeanor that coincide with a new friendship.

It's important to differentiate between occasional disagreements, which are a normal part of any friendship, and consistent negativity. Healthy friendships involve a balance of give and take, mutual respect, and support. Conversely, unhealthy friendships often lack these elements. Instead of mutual support, there might be a pattern of one friend dominating the relationship or consistently taking advantage of the other. Observe the power dynamics in the friendship— is your child consistently deferring to the other friend's wishes, even when they're uncomfortable? This could indicate an imbalance of power within the friendship, a hallmark of an unhealthy relationship.

Once you've identified potentially problematic friendships, the next step is to engage in thoughtful conversation with your preteen. Avoid accusatory language or directly attacking their friendship. Instead, focus on expressing your concerns with empathy and understanding.

For instance, you might say something like, "I've noticed you seem a little down lately after spending time with [friend's name]. Can we talk about what's going on?" This approach opens a dialogue without making your child feel defensive. Active listening is critical during this conversation. Listen attentively to their perspective and validate their feelings. Even if you disagree with their choices, demonstrating empathy allows for a more open and productive conversation.

It's crucial to avoid dismissing your preteen's feelings or downplaying the importance of their friendships. To them, these relationships are often incredibly significant, and dismissing their concerns can damage the trust and open communication you're trying to cultivate. Instead, aim to help your preteen analyze the situation objectively. Ask open-ended questions that encourage reflection. For example, "What are some of the things you enjoy about this friendship?" and "What are some of the challenges you've faced?" This allows them to articulate their feelings and critically evaluate the relationship's strengths and weaknesses.

Promoting positive peer interactions goes beyond simply identifying unhealthy friendships; it involves actively fostering healthy ones. Encourage participation in activities that promote social interaction and teamwork. Joining sports teams, clubs, or volunteer organizations can expose your preteen to diverse social circles and provide opportunities to develop social skills in a structured environment. These settings allow them to interact with peers who share common interests, fostering positive relationships based on shared values and activities.

Empathy is a vital social skill that plays a crucial role in building healthy relationships. Encourage your preteen to consider others' perspectives, emotions, and experiences.

This can be achieved through storytelling, role-playing, or discussions about social situations they might encounter. For example, you could present them with a hypothetical scenario: "Imagine your friend is feeling left out; how might that make them feel, and what could you do to help?" This helps them cultivate emotional intelligence and strengthens their ability to understand and respond to the feelings of others.

Respect for others is equally paramount. Teach your preteen about the importance of treating everyone with courtesy and consideration, regardless of differences in background, beliefs, or social status. Model respectful behavior in your own interactions, both at home and in public. This sets a positive example and demonstrates that respect is a fundamental principle in building positive relationships. Highlight situations where respect is shown, and discuss those instances where it's lacking. Open discussion helps solidify its importance.

Handling bullying and exclusion requires proactive strategies. Ensure your preteen knows that it is unacceptable to bully others, and explain that being the victim of bullying is not their fault. Teach assertive communication techniques to help them stand up for themselves or intervene when they see someone else being bullied. This could involve directly confronting the bully, reporting the incident to a trusted adult, or seeking help from friends or teachers. Rehearsing these scenarios through role-playing can build their confidence and preparedness.

Developing self-confidence is a significant aspect of navigating social dynamics successfully. Preteens who lack self-confidence may be more susceptible to peer pressure and less likely to assert their needs. Boosting their self-esteem through positive reinforcement, encouraging participation in activities they enjoy, and celebrating their accomplishments can significantly improve their social interactions and overall well-being. Helping them identify their strengths and talents empowers them to interact with others with increased confidence.

Prosocial behavior is about acting in a way that benefits others and contributes to the well-being of the community. Encourage acts of kindness, empathy, and cooperation. Participating in volunteer work, assisting family members with chores, or simply showing kindness to others fosters a sense of responsibility and social contribution. This strengthens their sense of community and builds positive relationships with their peers and adults.

Conflict resolution skills are invaluable in navigating the complexities of friendships. Inevitably, disagreements and conflicts arise. Teach your preteen strategies for resolving conflicts peacefully and constructively. This involves active listening, understanding different perspectives, compromising, and finding mutually agreeable solutions. Role-playing scenarios can help them practice these skills in a safe and controlled environment.

Building resilience helps preteens navigate the inevitable challenges of social interactions. Resilience is the ability to bounce back from adversity. By fostering a supportive and understanding environment at home, encouraging them to develop coping mechanisms, and providing positive feedback, you build their capacity to overcome social difficulties. This allows them to navigate setbacks without excessive emotional distress and maintains a positive outlook.

In conclusion, nurturing healthy friendships and developing positive social skills requires a multi-pronged approach. Parents must be actively involved in their children's social lives, helping them identify unhealthy friendships, promoting prosocial behaviors, and equipping them with the tools to navigate social challenges effectively. By fostering empathy, respect, self-confidence, and conflict-resolution skills, parents empower their preteens to build strong, meaningful, and supportive relationships that enhance their overall well-being and contribute to a positive social experience. Remember that open communication, active listening, and providing a safe space for sharing experiences are fundamental to your role in guiding your child towards a positive and successful social life. Continued support, understanding, and proactive engagement are essential throughout this developmental stage.

The digital age has profoundly reshaped the landscape of preteen social interactions, introducing both exciting opportunities and significant challenges. Social media platforms and various technological devices have become integral parts of their lives, influencing their friendships, self-perception, and overall well-being. Understanding this complex interplay is crucial for parents seeking to guide their children effectively. Navigating this terrain requires a balanced approach, recognizing the potential benefits while mitigating the risks associated with excessive or irresponsible technology use.

One of the most significant impacts of social media is its ability to expand social circles beyond geographical limitations. Preteens can connect with peers who share similar interests, regardless of their physical proximity. This can be particularly beneficial for children who may struggle to form friendships in traditional settings, offering them a sense of belonging and community. Online communities built around shared hobbies, academic subjects, or even online gaming can provide opportunities for social interaction and skill development. However, it's important to remember that online friendships, while valuable, differ significantly from in-person relationships. The lack of face-to-face interaction can lead to misunderstandings, misinterpretations, and a diminished sense of empathy. The curated nature of online profiles can also create unrealistic expectations and foster comparisons that negatively impact self-esteem.

Cyberbullying is a serious concern in the digital age, representing a significant threat to preteens' emotional well-being. Unlike traditional bullying, cyberbullying can occur anytime, anywhere, extending beyond the schoolyard and into the privacy of their homes. The anonymity offered by the internet can embolden bullies, leading to more frequent and severe incidents. The persistent nature of online harassment, with messages and images readily accessible for extended periods, can have a devastating impact on a preteen's self-worth and mental health. The public nature of some online platforms means that cyberbullying incidents can spread rapidly, causing widespread humiliation and distress. Parents need to be vigilant, monitoring their children's online activities and educating them about the potential risks of cyberbullying. Open communication is essential; children need to feel comfortable reporting any instances of online harassment to a trusted adult without fear of reprisal.

Online safety is paramount in the context of preteen social media use. Educating children about the dangers of sharing personal information online is critical. This includes their full name, address, phone number, school name, and any identifying details that could compromise their safety. Children need to understand the importance of privacy settings and the potential consequences of sharing sensitive information with strangers or individuals they don't know well. Parents should regularly discuss online safety with their children, reinforcing the importance of critical thinking and responsible online behavior. Open dialogue about appropriate online interactions is crucial, ensuring children understand the boundaries of acceptable online conduct.

Responsible technology use extends beyond merely avoiding online risks; it also involves establishing healthy habits and boundaries regarding screen time. Excessive technology use can negatively impact sleep patterns, physical health, and academic performance. Preteens may experience difficulties concentrating, reduced attention spans, and increased irritability due to excessive screen time. It's vital to establish clear guidelines regarding technology use, setting limits on screen time and creating designated technology-free zones within the home. These boundaries should be age-appropriate and adapted to the individual child's needs and maturity level. Consistent enforcement of these boundaries is essential to avoid conflicts and maintain healthy habits. Incorporating regular physical activity, outdoor playtime, and offline social interactions into their daily routines helps to create a balanced lifestyle that mitigates the negative effects of excessive screen time.

The impact of social media on self-esteem and mental health is a significant concern for preteens. The constant exposure to curated images and seemingly perfect lives presented on social media platforms can foster feelings of inadequacy and low self-worth. Preteens may engage in social comparison, evaluating themselves against unrealistic standards and feeling inadequate in comparison to their peers. This can lead to negative self-perception, body image issues, and a heightened sense of anxiety and depression. Open and honest conversations with preteens about the curated nature of social media and the importance of self-acceptance are crucial. Encouraging healthy self-esteem through positive reinforcement, focusing on their strengths and accomplishments, and promoting a balanced perspective on social media's influence is vital.

Parental involvement in their preteen's online world is not about controlling or monitoring every aspect of their digital lives; it's about guiding and educating them to make responsible choices. This involves fostering open communication, creating a safe space for them to discuss online experiences, and actively participating in conversations about online safety, responsible social media use, and potential risks. Parents should be aware of the platforms their children use, the types of content they engage with, and the individuals they interact with online. However, this should be approached with respect for their child's privacy and independence, striking a balance between supervision and trust. Constant monitoring can breed resentment and damage the parent-child relationship, while complete neglect leaves children vulnerable to the potential dangers of the online world.

The development of critical thinking skills is essential in navigating the complexities of the digital age. Preteens need to learn to evaluate information critically, distinguishing between factual and misleading content. They need to understand that social media often presents a skewed and unrealistic portrayal of reality, and they should be encouraged to approach online information with a healthy dose of skepticism. This includes recognizing the potential for manipulation and misinformation online, developing the ability to identify biased content, and forming their own informed opinions based on verified sources. Regular discussions about media literacy and critical thinking can equip preteens with the tools to navigate the digital landscape responsibly and safely.

Digital citizenship is another critical aspect of responsible technology use. Educating preteens about their rights and responsibilities as digital citizens is essential. This involves teaching them about ethical online behavior, respecting intellectual property rights, and avoiding plagiarism or unauthorized content sharing. They need to understand the consequences of their online actions and the importance of behaving responsibly and respectfully towards others in the digital world. Discussions about online etiquette, cyberbullying prevention, and the legal implications of online activities should be an integral part of their education. Promoting a sense of digital responsibility prepares them to navigate the challenges and opportunities presented by the online world with integrity and respect.

In conclusion, the role of social media and technology in the lives of preteens is multifaceted and complex. While these technologies offer numerous opportunities for social connection, learning, and entertainment, they also present significant risks. Parents must engage proactively, fostering open communication, setting clear expectations and boundaries, and educating their children about online safety, responsible technology use, and the potential impact on self-esteem and mental health. By equipping preteens with the necessary skills and knowledge, parents can empower them to navigate the digital landscape safely and responsibly, maximizing the benefits while minimizing the risks. A balanced approach, emphasizing both the opportunities and the challenges, is essential in fostering healthy development in this ever-evolving digital age. Remember, ongoing dialogue, adaptation to emerging technologies, and continued support are crucial to guiding your child through this dynamic phase of their lives.

The transition from childhood to adolescence is often marked by significant shifts in social dynamics. While some preteens thrive in social situations, others may struggle with social anxiety, leading to feelings of isolation and loneliness. This can manifest in various ways, from reluctance to participate in group activities to avoiding social gatherings altogether. For parents, witnessing their child grapple with social anxiety can be deeply concerning, prompting a natural desire to offer support and guidance. However, understanding the nuances of social anxiety in preteens is crucial for providing effective assistance. It's important to remember that shyness is a common trait, but social anxiety is a more significant concern when it interferes with a child's daily life, academic performance, and overall well-being.

One of the first steps in addressing social anxiety in preteens is recognizing the signs and symptoms. These can vary significantly from child to child, but common indicators include persistent worry about social situations, avoidance of social interactions, difficulty making and maintaining friendships, excessive self-consciousness, and fear of judgment or criticism. Physical symptoms, such as sweating, trembling, or rapid heartbeat, may also accompany social anxiety. It's crucial for parents to differentiate between typical shyness and a more significant anxiety disorder. While shyness might involve a brief feeling of discomfort in new social situations, social anxiety is characterized by more persistent and intense feelings of fear and apprehension that significantly impair a child's ability to function socially.

The root causes of social anxiety in preteens are complex and multifaceted. Genetic predisposition can play a significant role, with a family history of anxiety disorders increasing the likelihood of a child developing similar issues. Negative experiences, such as bullying, social exclusion, or traumatic events, can also contribute to the development of social anxiety. Perfectionistic tendencies and a fear of failure can also heighten social anxiety, leading children to avoid situations where they might make mistakes or feel judged. Negative self-perception and low self-esteem often accompany social anxiety, creating a vicious cycle of avoidance and negative reinforcement. Understanding these underlying factors is crucial for tailoring effective intervention strategies.

Providing support for a preteen struggling with social anxiety involves a multifaceted approach, encompassing emotional support, behavioral strategies, and, in some cases, professional intervention. Creating a safe and supportive home environment is paramount. This means fostering open communication, creating opportunities for the preteen to express their feelings without judgment, and validating their anxieties. Parents can help by actively listening, showing empathy, and demonstrating understanding of their child's struggles. Avoid minimizing or dismissing their concerns; instead, acknowledge the validity of their feelings and offer reassurance. Regular family time, engaging in shared activities, and creating opportunities for positive family interactions can reinforce feelings of security and belonging.

Behavioral strategies can also be remarkably effective in addressing social anxiety. Gradual exposure to social situations, starting with less anxiety-provoking scenarios and gradually progressing to more challenging ones, can help desensitize the child to social triggers. This could involve starting with small, comfortable interactions, such as inviting one friend over for a playdate, before progressing to larger group activities. Role-playing social situations can be beneficial, allowing the preteen to practice responses to challenging scenarios in a safe and supportive environment. Positive reinforcement for even small successes in social interactions can greatly boost confidence and encourage further engagement. Parents should celebrate small wins and emphasize the child's efforts rather than just focusing on outcomes.

Social skills training can be instrumental in equipping preteens with the tools necessary to navigate social interactions effectively. This might involve teaching active listening skills, encouraging appropriate eye contact, practicing initiating conversations, and learning how to respond to social cues. There are numerous resources available to support this, including books, workshops, and online programs designed to build social skills. Parents can play a crucial role by modeling appropriate social behaviors and offering guidance and encouragement as the preteen practices these skills. Positive feedback and praise reinforce their progress and build their confidence. Regular practice and patience are key to success in this area.

Collaboration with schools is essential in supporting preteens with social anxiety. Open communication between parents and teachers can ensure a consistent approach and provide a supportive learning environment. Schools can offer accommodations, such as allowing the preteen to participate in group activities at their own pace, providing extra time for assignments, or offering opportunities for quiet time when needed. Involving school counselors or therapists can provide additional support and guidance, creating a cohesive support network for the preteen. School staff can also help to identify and address any potential social stressors at school, such as bullying or social exclusion.

Seeking professional help is often a crucial step in addressing social anxiety, particularly when it significantly impacts a child's well-being. A therapist specializing in child and adolescent mental health can provide a comprehensive assessment, diagnose the underlying issues, and develop an individualized treatment plan. Therapy can involve cognitive behavioral therapy (CBT), which helps to identify and challenge negative thoughts and beliefs, and develop coping mechanisms for managing anxiety. Other therapeutic approaches, such as play therapy or family therapy, may also be beneficial depending on the child's specific needs. Early intervention is essential, as untreated social anxiety can have lasting consequences.

The importance of early intervention cannot be overstated. Addressing social anxiety in the early stages can prevent the development of more significant mental health issues later in life. Early intervention can also help to prevent the negative impact of social anxiety on academic performance, social relationships, and overall well-being. The sooner appropriate support is provided, the more likely it is that the preteen will develop healthy coping mechanisms and manage their anxiety effectively.

Access to support resources is crucial for parents and preteens. Many organizations offer valuable resources, including educational materials, support groups, and referral services. Online resources can provide information about social anxiety, treatment options, and support networks. Parent support groups can provide a valuable forum for sharing experiences and learning from others facing similar challenges. These resources can offer valuable support and guidance, helping parents to navigate the challenges of supporting a preteen with social anxiety.

In conclusion, supporting a preteen with social anxiety or isolation requires a multifaceted approach that combines emotional support, behavioral strategies, collaboration with schools, and professional help when needed. By creating a safe and supportive environment, teaching social skills, and promoting positive self-perception, parents can equip their child with the tools necessary to navigate social situations effectively. Early intervention, access to appropriate resources, and a collaborative approach involving parents, schools, and mental health professionals are essential for helping preteens overcome social anxiety and build healthy social relationships. Remember, patience, understanding, and unwavering support are vital in guiding preteens towards greater confidence and social well-being. The journey may have its ups and downs, but with persistence and the right support system, progress can be made, enabling the preteen to thrive socially and reach their full potential.

Chapter 4
Managing Family Dynamics and Conflicts

U nderstanding the intricate web of family relationships
and communication styles is crucial for navigating the
preteen years successfully. The family unit acts as a
microcosm of society, providing the foundational framework
for a child's social and emotional development. Preteens,
caught between childhood and adolescence, are particularly
sensitive to the nuances of family dynamics. Their perception
of family relationships significantly influences their self-
esteem, confidence, and ability to form healthy relationships
outside the home. A family's communication patterns, both
verbal and nonverbal, shape the overall atmosphere and
impact the child's emotional well-being.

Families exhibit diverse communication styles, each
with its unique strengths and weaknesses. Some families
embrace open and expressive communication, where family
members freely share their thoughts and feelings. This style
fosters a sense of trust and emotional intimacy, enabling
preteens to feel heard and understood. However, open
communication can also lead to conflict if not managed

constructively. Disagreements may arise, but the ability to resolve these conflicts respectfully and effectively is key to maintaining a healthy family dynamic.

In contrast, some families adopt a more restrained communication style, where emotional expression is limited, and conflicts are avoided or suppressed. While this approach might appear to maintain outward harmony, it can hinder emotional growth and create a climate of unspoken tension. Preteens in such families may struggle to express their needs and feelings, leading to internalized stress and potential emotional difficulties. The lack of open dialogue can also make it challenging to address conflicts effectively, leaving unresolved issues to fester and potentially escalate.

Another communication style prevalent in many families is the authoritarian approach. This style is characterized by a hierarchical structure, with parents holding primary authority and decision-making power. While this structure can offer a sense of stability and clear expectations, it can also stifle open communication and limit a preteen's opportunity for self-expression. Preteens may feel unheard or undervalued, potentially leading to resentment or rebellious behavior. Finding a balance between authority and open dialogue is essential in fostering a healthy parent-child relationship.

Furthermore, the concept of family systems theory helps to understand how each member of the family influences the others. A change in one family member's behavior can trigger a ripple effect, impacting the entire system. For example, a preteen's increased social anxiety might strain the family's dynamics, leading to increased parental worry and potential conflict between siblings.

Understanding this interconnectedness helps parents to approach challenges holistically, recognizing that addressing individual issues often necessitates a systemic approach.

Identifying recurring conflicts within the family system is another crucial aspect of understanding family dynamics. These conflicts often stem from underlying issues related to communication styles, unmet needs, or differing expectations. Common sources of conflict include disagreements over household chores, academic performance, screen time, social activities, and friendships. Understanding the root cause of these conflicts is essential for resolving them effectively. Simply addressing the surface-level issue may not be enough; delving deeper into the underlying emotions and unmet needs often reveals the true source of the conflict.

Once recurring conflicts are identified, parents can begin to address them using constructive communication techniques. Active listening, where parents genuinely listen and attempt to understand their preteen's perspective, is vital. Avoiding judgmental or dismissive responses is critical; instead, parents should validate their preteen's feelings and concerns. Empathetic responses demonstrate understanding and create a safe space for open dialogue. Using "I" statements, rather than accusatory "You" statements, can help to de-escalate conflict and facilitate productive conversation. For example, instead of saying, "You never help with chores," a parent could say, "I feel frustrated when chores aren't completed, and I would appreciate it if we could work together to find a solution."

Another effective communication strategy is compromise and negotiation. Parents should involve their preteen in the problem-solving process, allowing them to voice their opinions and contribute to finding a mutually agreeable solution. This demonstrates respect for their autonomy and empowers them to take ownership of their actions and choices. This collaborative approach fosters a sense of responsibility and shared decision-making, contributing to a more harmonious family environment.

Setting clear expectations and establishing consistent boundaries is crucial for managing family dynamics. Preteens thrive on structure and clear guidelines, providing them with a sense of security and predictability. These boundaries should be established collaboratively, involving the preteen in the discussion and allowing them to contribute to the rules that govern the family. This approach avoids creating a power struggle and fosters a sense of cooperation and shared responsibility.

Regular family meetings can serve as a valuable forum for open communication and conflict resolution. These meetings provide a designated time and space for family members to express their thoughts and concerns in a structured and respectful manner. Establishing ground rules for these meetings, such as respectful listening, taking turns speaking, and avoiding interruptions, can ensure that the discussions remain productive and constructive. Regular family meetings also create an environment where family members can check in with each other and build stronger connections.

Fostering positive family interactions is essential for building strong relationships and enhancing communication. Engaging in shared activities, such as family dinners, game nights, or outings, strengthens family bonds and creates opportunities for meaningful interactions. These shared experiences create lasting memories and promote a sense of belonging and connection. Even small gestures of appreciation and affection can go a long way in strengthening family relationships.

Furthermore, recognizing the importance of seeking professional help when needed is crucial. If family conflicts persist despite employing constructive communication strategies, seeking guidance from a family therapist or counselor can be immensely beneficial. A professional can provide objective insights into family dynamics, help identify underlying issues, and facilitate healthy communication patterns. Family therapy offers a structured setting for resolving conflicts and building stronger family relationships. It can help families to develop healthier communication strategies, learn how to resolve conflict constructively, and improve their overall family functioning.

In conclusion, understanding family systems and communication patterns is fundamental to navigating the challenges of the preteen years. By fostering open communication, employing constructive conflict-resolution strategies, and seeking professional help when necessary, parents can create a positive and supportive family environment where preteens can thrive. Building strong family relationships and effective communication skills will equip preteens with the tools they need to navigate their own relationships and challenges effectively, setting the stage for their successful transition to adolescence and beyond. The investment in healthy family dynamics is an investment in a child's future well-being and overall success.

Effective conflict resolution is not merely about silencing disagreements; it's about transforming disagreements into opportunities for growth and strengthening family bonds. Families, by their very nature, are comprised of individuals with unique perspectives, needs, and desires. These differences, while enriching, inevitably lead to conflicts. The key to navigating these conflicts lies not in avoiding them, but in developing effective strategies to resolve them constructively. This approach fosters an environment of mutual respect and understanding, where family members feel safe expressing themselves and working collaboratively towards solutions.

One of the most crucial aspects of effective conflict resolution is active listening. This goes beyond simply hearing words; it involves truly understanding the emotional context behind those words. Active listening requires paying close attention to both verbal and nonverbal cues, such as tone of voice, body language, and facial expressions. It means putting aside preconceived notions and judgments, and striving to see the situation from the other person's perspective. When a family member feels truly heard and understood, they are more likely to be receptive to finding a resolution. To enhance active listening skills, parents can utilize reflective listening techniques, paraphrasing what their child has said to ensure understanding and demonstrating empathy. For example, instead of interrupting or offering solutions immediately, a parent might say, "So, it sounds like you're feeling frustrated because..." This validates the child's feelings and creates a safe space for open communication.

Empathy plays a critical role in de-escalating arguments and promoting respectful dialogue. Empathy involves understanding and sharing the feelings of another person. When parents demonstrate empathy, they convey a message of understanding and support, helping to reduce defensiveness and animosity. This doesn't mean agreeing with every perspective, but rather acknowledging and validating the emotions behind those perspectives. For instance, if a preteen is upset about a curfew, a parent can respond with empathy by saying, "I understand you're disappointed about the curfew. It feels restricting to you, and I want you to know that I hear you." This acknowledgment of the child's feelings can significantly de-escalate the situation and pave the way for a more productive conversation.

Compromise and negotiation are essential components of finding mutually agreeable solutions. Conflict resolution isn't about winning or losing; it's about finding a solution that works for everyone involved. This requires a willingness to compromise and negotiate, to find common ground and create a win-win situation. Involving the preteen in the problem-solving process empowers them and fosters a sense of responsibility. For example, if there's a disagreement about screen time, parents can involve their preteen in creating a schedule that balances their entertainment needs with other responsibilities. This collaborative approach helps foster a sense of ownership and commitment to the solution.

Setting clear and consistent boundaries is another critical aspect of effective conflict resolution. Boundaries define acceptable behavior and help prevent conflicts from escalating. These boundaries should be established collaboratively, involving the preteen in the discussion to ensure they understand and agree with the rules. The process of setting boundaries should be viewed as a collaborative effort, not a dictatorial one. When boundaries are clear and consistently enforced, preteens know what to expect and are less likely to engage in behaviors that lead to conflict. Clear boundaries foster a sense of security and predictability, reducing anxiety and promoting a more harmonious family environment. For example, establishing consistent bedtimes, chore expectations, and rules regarding screen time can minimize future conflicts. It's vital to explain the rationale behind these boundaries, fostering a sense of understanding and reducing the potential for conflict.

"I" statements are a powerful tool for communicating feelings and needs without placing blame. Instead of using accusatory "you" statements, which can be perceived as attacks, "I" statements focus on personal feelings and experiences. For example, instead of saying, "You always leave your room messy," a parent might say, "I feel frustrated when I see the room messy because it makes it difficult to keep the house tidy." This approach is less likely to provoke defensiveness and is more likely to lead to a constructive dialogue. This technique shifts the focus from blame to personal feelings, opening up the possibility for collaborative problem-solving. Modeling this type of communication is essential; children learn by observing their parents' communication styles.

Regular family meetings can provide a designated time and space for open communication and conflict resolution. These meetings should be held regularly, perhaps weekly or bi-weekly, to prevent small issues from escalating into larger conflicts. During these meetings, family members can express their feelings, concerns, and needs in a structured and supportive environment. Establishing ground rules for the meetings, such as respectful listening and taking turns speaking, can ensure productive discussions. These meetings also foster a sense of unity and collaboration, creating a space for shared decision-making. The family meeting isn't just for resolving conflicts; it's also an opportunity to celebrate successes, plan family activities, and maintain strong connections.

Understanding the root cause of conflicts is crucial for effective resolution. Surface-level arguments often mask underlying issues related to unmet needs, differing values, or communication breakdowns. Therefore, it's crucial to delve beneath the surface and explore the deeper emotions and needs fueling the conflict. For example, a child's resistance to chores might stem from feeling overwhelmed or undervalued. Addressing the underlying feelings of being overwhelmed, rather than simply focusing on the undone chores, would likely yield more productive results. Open-ended questions, such as "Tell me more about why you're feeling this way," can help uncover these underlying issues.

Forgiveness is an essential component of effective conflict resolution. Holding onto resentment and anger prevents moving forward and repairing relationships. Forgiveness doesn't necessarily mean condoning the behavior that caused the conflict, but rather letting go of the negative emotions associated with it. This is a crucial process for both parents and children to learn and practice. It allows for healing and the rebuilding of trust. Practicing forgiveness, even in small ways, can significantly improve family dynamics and interpersonal relationships.

In instances where families struggle to resolve conflicts independently, seeking professional help is a sign of strength, not weakness. A family therapist can provide objective guidance, help identify underlying issues, and teach effective communication strategies. Therapy provides a safe and structured environment for families to work through their difficulties and develop healthier communication patterns. It's a valuable resource for improving family dynamics and fostering stronger relationships. There is no shame in seeking professional assistance, as it often leads to significant improvements in family functioning and overall well-being.

Finally, maintaining a positive and supportive family atmosphere is crucial for preventing and resolving conflicts. Engaging in shared activities, celebrating successes, and expressing appreciation can strengthen family bonds and promote a sense of belonging. Small acts of kindness, such as expressing gratitude or offering a helping hand, can significantly impact family dynamics. These positive interactions foster a sense of connection and create a more resilient family unit, better equipped to navigate inevitable conflicts. Building strong family relationships is a continuous process that requires time, effort, and a commitment to fostering understanding and empathy among all family members. The rewards, however, are immeasurable, creating a supportive and nurturing environment where preteens can flourish.

Sibling rivalry is a common experience in families with multiple children, often stemming from competition for parental attention, resources, and affection. While some level of conflict is normal and even healthy in its development of social skills, persistent or intense sibling rivalry can significantly disrupt family harmony and negatively impact each child's emotional well-being. Understanding the underlying causes of sibling rivalry is the first step toward effective management.

One major contributor is the inherent competition for parental attention. Preteens, especially, are navigating significant developmental changes and increased independence. They might perceive their siblings as rivals for parental approval, love, and time, leading to jealousy and resentment. This competition is often intensified during milestones such as the arrival of a new sibling, academic achievements, or social successes. For example, a preteen might feel overlooked when a younger sibling receives praise for a seemingly minor accomplishment. Similarly, a preteen who excels academically might feel their achievements are undervalued if their sibling's artistic talents garner more parental attention. Recognizing this inherent drive for attention is crucial in mitigating conflict.

Another contributing factor is the unequal distribution of resources. This can manifest in various ways, from unequal division of chores to perceived favoritism in allocating privileges like screen time, access to toys, or participation in family outings. Even seemingly minor disparities can ignite intense sibling rivalry. A preteen who feels unfairly treated might resort to aggressive behaviors, such as teasing, name-calling, or physical aggression, to express their frustration and attempt to regain a sense of balance or perceived fairness. Parents should strive to ensure fairness in resource allocation as much as possible. This does not necessarily mean strict equality, as children have different needs and developmental stages. However, open communication about resource distribution and the rationale behind decisions is essential.

Differing personalities and temperaments also contribute to sibling rivalry. Children are naturally diverse. One child may be outgoing and assertive, while another is shy and introverted. These differences can create friction, leading to misunderstandings and conflicts. An assertive preteen might dominate interactions, leaving a more passive sibling feeling unheard or overlooked. Conversely, a shy preteen might struggle to express their needs and desires, leading to resentment and frustration that manifests as passive-aggressive behaviors. Parents need to understand and respect each child's unique personality while encouraging them to develop effective communication skills.

The impact of parental behavior cannot be underestimated. Parents often unintentionally fuel sibling rivalry through favoritism, inconsistent discipline, or ineffective conflict resolution strategies. Perceived favoritism, even if unintentional, can create significant resentment and drive a wedge between siblings. Inconsistent discipline, where one child is held to stricter standards than another, breeds unfairness and fosters conflict. Ineffective conflict resolution strategies, such as siding with one child over another or ignoring the conflict altogether, allow disagreements to escalate, further damaging sibling relationships.

Effective management of sibling rivalry requires a multi-faceted approach that encompasses several key strategies. First, parents need to actively promote empathy and understanding between siblings. This involves encouraging them to see things from each other's perspectives. Activities that foster empathy, such as role-playing or reading stories about sibling relationships, can help children understand each other's feelings and motivations. Encouraging them to express their feelings and needs using "I" statements can diffuse conflicts before they escalate into larger arguments. "I feel frustrated when you use my things without asking," is far more productive than "You always take my stuff!"

Secondly, establishing clear rules and expectations for behavior is crucial. These rules should be collaboratively developed with the children, ensuring that they understand and agree with the boundaries. Consistency in enforcing these rules is essential for preventing future conflicts. Consequences for breaking the rules should be fair and consistent for both siblings. Parents should avoid playing favorites and instead focus on creating a sense of fairness and equality. A clearly defined set of rules regarding sharing, personal space, and conflict resolution techniques can mitigate future problems. It's important to be consistent not only with enforcement but also with communication surrounding these rules.

Teaching children effective conflict resolution skills is vital in managing sibling rivalry. This involves providing them with tools and techniques to resolve disagreements peacefully and constructively. This includes teaching active listening skills, such as summarizing or paraphrasing what their sibling has said. It also includes techniques such as brainstorming together for solutions, compromising, and finding mutually agreeable solutions. These skills can be taught and practiced through games and role-playing scenarios which allow the child to practice their skills in a safe and supportive environment. The goal isn't to eliminate all conflicts, but rather to teach children how to manage them effectively and reach constructive resolutions.

Regular family meetings can be incredibly beneficial in fostering positive communication and conflict resolution. These meetings provide a designated time and space for family members to express their feelings, concerns, and needs in a structured environment. The meetings should focus on establishing clear expectations and working collaboratively to solve problems. Family meetings are a preventative tool, helping to address issues before they escalate into major conflicts. They also foster a sense of collaboration and strengthen family bonds. It's important that the family meetings feel like a safe space for open communication rather than an interrogation.

Another crucial strategy is to foster individual time and attention for each child. This is especially important for preteens who are seeking increased independence and a stronger sense of self. Parents should make an effort to spend quality time alone with each child, engaging in activities that the child enjoys. This shows the child that they are valued and loved individually, which mitigates feelings of competition and jealousy. Individual time allows parents to connect on a deeper level, understand their child's unique needs, and nurture their individual growth. This dedicated time should not be seen as a reward for good behavior but rather as a fundamental aspect of nurturing a healthy parent-child relationship.

Fairness does not necessarily mean equal treatment. Children have different needs and temperaments, which should be considered when addressing their conflicts and distributing resources. What might feel fair to one child might feel unfair to the other. The key is to establish transparent and consistent criteria for decision-making, openly communicating those reasons to each child. Understanding the underlying emotions and needs driving their behavior is also critical. If a child is acting out due to feeling overlooked, the focus should be on addressing their underlying emotional needs, not just suppressing the problematic behavior.

In some cases, professional help may be necessary. If sibling rivalry is significantly impacting the family's well-being, a family therapist can provide objective guidance and teach effective conflict resolution strategies. A therapist can help families identify underlying issues that are contributing to the conflicts and develop strategies for managing them effectively. They can also help siblings communicate more effectively and learn to understand each other's perspectives. Seeking professional help should not be viewed as a sign of failure, but rather a proactive step in creating a healthier and happier family environment.

Finally, parents should prioritize fostering a positive and supportive family atmosphere. This involves engaging in shared activities, expressing appreciation, and celebrating successes as a family. Small gestures of kindness and affection, such as expressing gratitude or offering help, can significantly impact family dynamics. Creating a warm and loving environment reduces feelings of insecurity and competition, and makes it more likely that siblings can find ways to cooperate and get along. A strong family unit is better equipped to handle the inevitable conflicts that arise in any family. Creating a secure and loving environment will provide the foundation for healthy sibling relationships that will endure throughout their lives. Consistent nurturing and empathy from parents creates a resilient family unit capable of navigating challenges together.

Maintaining open communication within a family unit is crucial at all times, but it becomes paramount during periods of significant stress. Events such as divorce, serious illness, job loss, or the death of a loved one can profoundly impact family dynamics, and the way parents communicate during these times significantly influences a preteen's emotional well-being and resilience. The key lies in adapting communication strategies to the specific circumstances, ensuring the message is clear, empathetic, and developmentally appropriate.

Divorce, for instance, often represents a seismic shift in a preteen's life. The familiar structure of their family is disrupted, potentially leading to feelings of insecurity, anxiety, and even anger. Open communication during this period is paramount. Parents should avoid using derogatory language about the other parent in front of the child. Children should be informed of the situation in age-appropriate language, avoiding overly detailed explanations that might overwhelm them. Explaining the reasons behind the separation in simple terms, focusing on the parents' decision to live apart but not diminishing the love for the child, is crucial. Reassuring the child that they are loved and will continue to receive the same level of support and care from both parents is essential. Creating a consistent routine and maintaining familiar aspects of their life, such as school schedules and extracurricular activities, helps to provide a sense of stability during this turbulent time. Regular, scheduled contact with both parents should be established and consistently maintained.

It's vital to actively listen to the preteen's concerns and validate their feelings. Their emotions might range from sadness and confusion to anger and resentment. Allowing them to express these feelings without judgment is critical. Encouraging them to ask questions and providing honest, age-appropriate answers can help to alleviate anxiety and promote a sense of security. Open dialogue helps the child process their emotions and feel heard. Creating a safe space where they feel comfortable sharing their thoughts and feelings without fear of reprimand is paramount to their healing process. This might involve regular one-on-one time with each parent, ensuring each child receives individual attention.

Similarly, dealing with a serious illness within the family demands careful and sensitive communication. Depending on the child's age and understanding of the illness, parents need to adapt their approach. Providing honest, age-appropriate information helps the preteen understand the situation without causing undue fear or anxiety. They should be included in age-appropriate discussions about the illness and treatment plan. This may involve explaining medical procedures in simple terms, or explaining that a family member may be experiencing physical or emotional challenges and needs extra support. The child's role in supporting the family, such as helping with simple chores, can give them a sense of purpose and participation during a challenging time. Openly acknowledging the emotional impact of the illness on the family, including the child's own feelings, creates a sense of shared experience and prevents the child from feeling isolated. Regular family meetings, if appropriate, can help maintain open dialogue and address concerns.

Job loss can also significantly impact family dynamics. The financial stress and emotional burden can create tension, affecting communication within the family. Parents should address the situation with honesty, explaining the circumstances to the preteen without causing undue alarm. Reassuring the child that their basic needs will be met, while remaining transparent about the family's adjustments, fosters a sense of security. Engaging the preteen in age-appropriate conversations about budgeting and making responsible choices teaches financial literacy while also providing a sense of involvement and responsibility. This involves discussing possible changes to the family budget or lifestyle that might affect them directly, and involving them in decisions in ways that are relevant to their age and abilities.

In the event of a significant loss, such as the death of a loved one, it's critical to approach communication with even greater sensitivity. Acknowledging the grief and allowing the preteen to express their feelings freely is paramount. Parents must respond to the child's specific emotional responses, and may find that it is necessary to seek out additional support. Explain death in age-appropriate terms. For younger preteens, simple explanations suffice, emphasizing that death is a natural part of life. For older preteens, more in-depth discussions might be necessary, depending on their maturity level and understanding. Creating rituals, such as writing letters to the deceased or planting a tree in their memory, can provide a healthy outlet for grief. Allowing space for the child's feelings—sadness, anger, or confusion—to surface and providing a nonjudgmental listening ear is vital. Seeking professional support from grief counselors or therapists can provide additional tools for coping with grief during this challenging time.

Maintaining a stable and supportive environment is essential during all these challenging times. This involves creating a consistent routine, providing opportunities for relaxation and fun, and ensuring adequate sleep and nutrition. Engaging in shared activities, even simple ones like family game night or movie night, can help maintain a sense of normalcy and strengthen family bonds. Expressing appreciation and celebrating small victories can significantly boost morale and foster a sense of unity.

Throughout these periods of stress, it's important to emphasize the significance of self-care for parents as well. Parents who are struggling to cope with stress are less equipped to provide emotional support to their children. Parents need to take time for themselves, engage in activities that promote relaxation and well-being, and seek support from friends, family, or professionals. Prioritizing self-care will enable them to navigate challenging times more effectively and better support their children.

Finally, recognizing when professional help is needed is crucial. If a preteen's emotional well-being is significantly affected, or if parents are struggling to cope effectively, seeking support from a child psychologist, family therapist, or counselor is a sign of strength, not weakness. These professionals can provide objective guidance, teach effective coping mechanisms, and help the family navigate the challenges they are facing. A professional can offer tools and strategies for managing emotional responses, improving communication, and fostering resilience. They can also help parents develop effective strategies for communicating with their preteens during challenging times. Remember, seeking help is a sign of proactive parenting and an investment in the long-term well-being of the entire family. Professional support provides access to valuable resources and creates a safer environment for both children and parents to navigate difficult situations. It allows for a more thorough and effective approach to healing and building resilience.

Creating a positive and supportive family environment is the bedrock of healthy preteen development. It's a space where open communication thrives, where individual needs are acknowledged, and where a strong sense of belonging fosters resilience. This isn't simply about avoiding conflict; it's about proactively cultivating an atmosphere of empathy, understanding, and mutual respect. This requires conscious effort and a commitment from all family members. One crucial aspect is establishing clear, consistent, and age-appropriate expectations. Preteens crave structure and predictability; it provides a sense of security in a world that's rapidly changing. This structure should not be rigid, but rather a framework that allows for flexibility and individual needs. For example, establishing regular family dinner times, even if it's just a couple of times a week, provides a designated space for conversation and connection.

Beyond routine, actively listening to your preteen is paramount. Truly hearing their perspective, without interrupting or judging, shows respect and builds trust. This means putting down your phone, making eye contact, and focusing on what they're saying, both verbally and nonverbally. Encourage them to express their thoughts and feelings, even if they seem trivial or insignificant to you. Sometimes, what might seem like a minor issue to an adult can be a significant source of stress or anxiety for a preteen. By validating their emotions, you help them feel understood and supported. For instance, if they are upset about a conflict with a friend, resist the urge to immediately offer solutions. Instead, start by acknowledging their feelings, saying something like, "It sounds like you're really hurt and frustrated by what happened with your friend. Tell me more about it."

Fostering a sense of belonging within the family is equally critical. This means creating opportunities for shared experiences and activities that cater to everyone's interests. These don't have to be elaborate or expensive. Simple activities like family game nights, movie nights, weekend hikes, or even just cooking dinner together can create lasting memories and strengthen family bonds. The key is to engage in activities that everyone enjoys, promoting inclusivity and a sense of shared accomplishment. Furthermore, actively celebrating accomplishments, both big and small, creates a positive feedback loop and encourages further growth. This may be a good grade on a test, a successful sports game, or even mastering a new skill, like riding a bike or playing a musical instrument.

Another significant aspect of creating a supportive environment is promoting individual autonomy within the family structure. Preteens are developing their independence and exploring their identity. Allowing them age-appropriate choices and responsibilities fosters a sense of self-efficacy and promotes their personal growth. This could involve letting them choose their own clothes (within reasonable limits), participating in family decision-making, or taking on age-appropriate chores around the house. These acts of independence build confidence and self-esteem. However, it is vital to balance this autonomy with appropriate boundaries.

Clear expectations and consequences for actions help preteens learn responsibility and navigate the complexities of their growing independence. Establishing consistent bedtimes, curfew times, and rules regarding technology use provide structure and prevent conflicts. Remember to communicate these expectations clearly and consistently, providing reasons and allowing for questions.

Regular family meetings can be a valuable tool for open communication and conflict resolution. These meetings should be conducted in a relaxed and informal setting, focusing on creating a space for open dialogue. Establish ground rules that encourage respectful communication and active listening. Ensure everyone has an opportunity to share their thoughts and feelings without interruption. This is a space where family members can voice their concerns, discuss challenges, and collaboratively brainstorm solutions. Furthermore, it is important to ensure these meetings don't become solely focused on problems. It's crucial to incorporate positive elements into these gatherings, sharing successes and celebrating achievements.

Creating a positive family environment also means prioritizing self-care for parents. It's impossible to provide consistent emotional support and guidance to your preteen if you're neglecting your own well-being. Parents need to schedule time for themselves, engage in activities that promote relaxation and rejuvenation, and ensure they're prioritizing their physical and mental health. This might involve pursuing hobbies, exercising regularly, getting enough sleep, eating healthy, and maintaining social connections with friends and family. Remember, self-care is not selfish; it's essential for effective parenting. Taking care of your own mental health will significantly impact your ability to respond patiently, supportively and effectively to your preteen.

Crucially, recognizing when to seek professional help is a sign of strength, not weakness. If you're struggling to manage conflicts, if communication consistently breaks down, or if your preteen is exhibiting significant emotional distress, don't hesitate to reach out to a family therapist, child psychologist, or counselor. These professionals can provide valuable tools and strategies for improving communication, conflict resolution, and family dynamics. They can also help assess whether there are any underlying issues contributing to family difficulties, and offer strategies to help you address these more effectively.

Cultivating a positive and supportive family environment is an ongoing process, not a destination. It requires consistent effort, patience, and a willingness to adapt to the ever-changing dynamics of family life. It's about creating a safe space where preteens feel loved, respected, and understood. This will involve actively nurturing open communication, promoting a sense of belonging, and establishing clear and consistent expectations. In doing so, you will not only help your preteen navigate the challenges of adolescence, but you will also build strong, lasting bonds that will enrich the lives of everyone in the family. Remember, this journey is as much about the parents' growth as it is about the child's, fostering resilience and adaptability in everyone involved. It's an investment that will yield immeasurable rewards as your preteen blossoms into a confident and well-adjusted young adult. By actively working to improve your family dynamics, you are creating the foundation for positive relationships and a happier future for your entire family. The effort you put in now will profoundly impact the future strength and well-being of your family unit.

Chapter 5:
Addressing Behavioral Challenges

U nderstanding and addressing defiance and opposition in preteens requires a shift in perspective from viewing these behaviors as intentional acts of rebellion to recognizing them as potential manifestations of underlying emotional and developmental needs. Preteens are navigating a complex period of significant physical, cognitive, and emotional changes. Their brains are undergoing rewiring, impacting their emotional regulation, impulse control, and decision-making abilities. This period, often characterized by mood swings and unpredictable behavior, can be incredibly challenging for both preteens and their parents.

Defiance, often expressed as outright refusal to comply with requests or rules, is a common behavior during preadolescence. It's crucial to understand that defiance is rarely a deliberate attempt to upset parents. Instead, it frequently stems from a desire for autonomy and independence. Preteens are striving to establish their own identity, separate from their parents, and asserting their independence, even in small ways, is a crucial part of this process. This doesn't mean that their actions should be condoned, but rather that their motivations need to be understood and addressed constructively. The key is to find ways to support their growing autonomy without compromising safety or family rules.

Oppositional behavior, characterized by a persistent pattern of arguing, defying authority, and intentionally annoying others, often stems from deeper-seated emotional issues. While some level of opposition is normal during preadolescence, consistent and excessive opposition warrants attention. It might be a manifestation of underlying anxiety, depression, or other emotional challenges. Ignoring or dismissing these behaviors can be detrimental, exacerbating the problem and damaging the parent-child relationship. Instead, proactive intervention and open communication are essential.

Irritability, characterized by frequent outbursts of anger, frustration, and easily triggered negative emotions, is another common behavioral challenge during this developmental stage. The hormonal changes that accompany puberty, coupled with the emotional turmoil of navigating social pressures, academic demands, and the changing dynamics of family life, can contribute to heightened irritability. Understanding the underlying triggers of their irritability is crucial. It's not merely about managing the behavior but about addressing the root causes. Open communication, active listening, and exploring the possible triggers behind these emotional outbursts can help alleviate this challenge.

Effective communication is the cornerstone of addressing these behavioral challenges. Rather than resorting to punishment or power struggles, which often escalate the situation and damage the parent-child relationship, focus on collaborative problem-solving and empathetic understanding. Begin by actively listening to your preteen's perspective. Create a safe space where they feel comfortable expressing their thoughts and feelings without judgment or interruption. Truly hearing their perspective, even if you don't agree with it, demonstrates respect and fosters trust. This doesn't mean you have to give in to their demands; rather, it's about validating their emotions and fostering a sense of being heard.

When addressing defiant or oppositional behavior, avoid engaging in power struggles. These rarely resolve the underlying issue and often damage the relationship. Instead, try to find common ground and collaborate on solutions. For example, instead of demanding they clean their room, engage in a conversation about the importance of maintaining a clean and organized space. Discuss the benefits, such as a more comfortable living environment and increased peace of mind. Involve them in the decision-making process, allowing them a degree of control and ownership over the situation.

Empathy is critical in navigating these difficult interactions. Try to understand the situation from your preteen's perspective. Consider the developmental stage they are in and the pressures they face. Often, their seemingly defiant or oppositional behavior stems from feeling overwhelmed, misunderstood, or powerless. Expressing empathy, acknowledging their feelings, and validating their experiences can help de-escalate the situation and foster a more collaborative approach. Phrases like, "I understand you're feeling frustrated," or "It sounds like you're really upset about this," can create a more receptive environment for communication.

Setting clear and consistent boundaries is crucial, but these boundaries should be established collaboratively whenever possible. Rather than imposing rules unilaterally, involve your preteen in the process of establishing expectations. This allows them a sense of control and ownership, making them more likely to adhere to the rules. When boundaries are violated, focus on natural consequences rather than punitive measures. For instance, if they fail to complete their chores, the natural consequence might be losing screen time or being unable to participate in a planned activity.

Positive reinforcement and encouragement are far more effective than punishment in shaping positive behaviors. Focus on rewarding desired behaviors, such as cooperation, responsibility, and respectful communication. This might involve verbal praise, extra privileges, or small rewards. Celebrate their successes, however small, to reinforce positive behaviors and build their self-esteem. By acknowledging their positive actions, you are creating a feedback loop that encourages further positive behavior.

It's crucial to remember that preteens are still developing their emotional regulation skills. They may not always be able to manage their emotions effectively, leading to outbursts of anger or defiance. Patience and understanding are vital during these moments. Providing them with strategies for managing their emotions, such as deep breathing exercises or mindfulness techniques, can equip them with tools to navigate their feelings more effectively. You can also model these strategies yourself, showing them how to effectively manage your own emotional responses in challenging situations.

If you're consistently struggling to manage your preteen's defiant or oppositional behavior, or if you suspect underlying emotional or mental health issues, don't hesitate to seek professional help. A family therapist, child psychologist, or counselor can provide valuable support and guidance. They can help assess whether there are underlying emotional or behavioral issues, and develop tailored strategies for addressing these challenges. They can also provide you with tools and techniques to improve your communication and conflict-resolution skills, strengthening your family relationships.

In summary, understanding and addressing defiance and opposition in preteens requires a multifaceted approach that prioritizes empathy, open communication, and collaborative problem-solving. By recognizing the developmental context of their behavior, providing them with emotional support, and setting clear but collaboratively established boundaries, you can navigate these challenging years and foster a strong and healthy parent-child relationship. Remember, this is a phase, and with patience, understanding, and the right approach, you can guide your preteen through this period of growth and development, helping them to become a confident and responsible young adult. Seeking professional help is not a sign of failure, but rather a proactive step toward creating a more supportive and healthy family environment. The investment in professional guidance can yield profound and lasting positive changes in your family dynamics, improving communication, reducing conflict, and ultimately fostering stronger relationships. This proactive approach can significantly enhance the well-being of both parents and the preteen, leading to a more harmonious and fulfilling family life.

Managing anger and emotional outbursts in preteens requires a nuanced approach that goes beyond simply suppressing outward expressions. It necessitates understanding the underlying causes of these outbursts and equipping preteens with the emotional intelligence and coping mechanisms to navigate their feelings constructively. The hormonal fluctuations of puberty significantly impact emotional regulation, leading to heightened sensitivity and increased susceptibility to emotional volatility. Add to this the social pressures of navigating friendships, academic challenges, and the ever-shifting dynamics of family life, and it becomes clear why emotional outbursts are so common during the preteen years.

The first step is to help your preteen identify and understand their emotions. This involves teaching emotional vocabulary—going beyond simple terms like "happy" and "sad" to explore the nuances of feelings like frustration, anxiety, disappointment, and resentment. Encourage your preteen to articulate their feelings using specific language. Instead of simply saying "I'm mad," encourage them to describe what's making them angry, what physical sensations they're experiencing (e.g., clenched fists, rapid heartbeat), and how those feelings affect their behavior. This process of emotional labeling helps to normalize their feelings and create a space for healthy emotional processing.

Visual aids, such as emotion charts or feeling wheels, can be helpful tools for younger preteens in learning to identify and label their emotions. These resources provide a visual representation of a range of emotions, helping them connect words with feelings. Interactive games or activities focusing on emotional identification can also make this learning experience more engaging and less intimidating. For older preteens, journaling can become a valuable tool for reflecting on their emotions and identifying triggers.

Once your preteen can identify their emotions, the next step is to teach them healthy coping mechanisms. These mechanisms should be age-appropriate and tailored to their individual needs and personality. Deep breathing exercises, for instance, are a simple yet effective way to calm down during moments of heightened emotion. Guided meditation or mindfulness exercises can help them focus on the present moment, reducing the intensity of their feelings. Physical activity, such as a brisk walk, a bike ride, or a workout, can be a great way to release pent-up energy and reduce stress. Creative outlets, such as drawing, painting, writing, or playing music, can provide a healthy way to express emotions.

For preteens who struggle with intense anger, learning anger management techniques is crucial. This could involve teaching them to count to ten, take deep breaths, or find a quiet space to calm down when they feel angry. Role-playing different scenarios can help them practice managing their anger in a controlled environment. It's important to teach them strategies for de-escalating the situation before it escalates into an outburst.

Empathy plays a crucial role in managing emotional outbursts. Encourage your preteen to consider the perspectives of others. Ask questions like, "How do you think your actions made [other person] feel?" or "What could you have done differently?" This helps them develop empathy and understand the impact of their behavior on others. Modeling empathetic behavior is equally important. Show your preteen how you manage your own emotions and how you consider the feelings of others in your interactions.

Non-violent communication (NVC) is a valuable framework for teaching preteens how to express their feelings constructively. NVC emphasizes expressing needs and feelings without blaming or criticizing others. It involves four key components: observing the situation objectively, identifying the feelings associated with the situation, expressing the underlying needs driving those feelings, and making a concrete request. For example, instead of saying, "You always leave your things everywhere, it's so frustrating!" using NVC, they would express: "I noticed my room is messy. I feel overwhelmed and frustrated. I need a clean and organized space to relax. Would you be willing to help me clean up?"

Open and honest communication is essential. Create a safe space where your preteen feels comfortable sharing their feelings without judgment or fear of reprimand. Listen actively to their concerns, validate their emotions, and demonstrate understanding even when you don't agree with their perspective. Regular family meetings can provide a structured environment for discussing concerns, resolving conflicts, and fostering open communication.

While positive reinforcement is key, setting clear and consistent boundaries is also vital. These boundaries should be age-appropriate and tailored to your family's values. Communicate these boundaries clearly and consistently, ensuring your preteen understands the consequences of violating them. Consequences should be logical and related to the behavior. For example, if a preteen damages property in an angry outburst, they might be required to help repair the damage or lose privileges until they demonstrate better control.

Remember, consistency is key. Be patient and persistent in your efforts to help your preteen manage their anger and emotional outbursts. It's a process, not a quick fix. It requires consistent effort from both parents and the preteen. Celebrate successes, no matter how small, to reinforce positive behavior.

Seeking professional help is not a sign of weakness or failure. If you're struggling to manage your preteen's emotional outbursts, consider seeking the support of a therapist or counselor specializing in adolescent development. They can provide valuable guidance, strategies, and tools to navigate these challenges more effectively, enhancing communication and fostering a healthier family dynamic. A therapist can also help rule out underlying conditions that may be contributing to the outbursts, such as anxiety, depression, or ADHD. They can work with the entire family to improve communication and conflict resolution skills, creating a more supportive and understanding environment. This professional guidance can empower both the parents and the preteen, creating a more harmonious and fulfilling family life.

It's important to remember that managing anger and emotional outbursts is an ongoing process. It requires patience, understanding, and consistent effort from both parents and the preteen. By implementing these strategies and seeking support when needed, you can help your preteen develop healthy coping mechanisms and navigate the emotional challenges of adolescence with greater confidence and resilience. This process fosters a strong parent-child bond and lays the foundation for a healthier and happier future. The journey may have its ups and downs, but with perseverance and a commitment to understanding and support, you can guide your preteen towards a more emotionally mature and balanced life. Remember that celebrating small victories and acknowledging progress, even on challenging days, is a crucial component of this process, helping to build the preteen's confidence and self-esteem. This positive reinforcement motivates them to continue practicing the techniques and strategies learned, reinforcing the development of healthy emotional regulation skills. Through consistent effort and unwavering support, you'll help your preteen navigate this critical developmental stage and emerge stronger and more resilient.

Lying and dishonesty are common challenges during the preteen years, a phase marked by significant developmental shifts and a growing desire for independence. Understanding the underlying reasons for these behaviors is crucial before implementing effective strategies. Preteens may lie to avoid punishment, escape responsibility, or impress their peers. Sometimes, a lie might stem from a desire to protect themselves or someone else, even if unintentionally. In other cases, it could be a way to navigate complex social situations where honesty might lead to social repercussions. The development of a strong moral compass is an ongoing process, and preteens may not always grasp the consequences of their actions.

Before addressing the lie itself, it's essential to create a safe and non-judgmental environment. A preteen who feels constantly criticized or threatened is more likely to resort to dishonesty to avoid confrontation. Instead of launching into an immediate interrogation or accusatory tone, strive for a calm and understanding approach. Start by acknowledging that you've noticed a discrepancy, rather than directly accusing them of lying. For example, instead of saying, "You lied to me about where you were last night," try saying, "I'm a little confused about the timeline of events last night. Can you help me understand?" This softer approach reduces defensiveness and increases the likelihood of an honest response.

Active listening is paramount. Give your preteen your undivided attention, making eye contact and demonstrating genuine interest in what they have to say. Avoid interrupting or dismissing their perspective. Even if their explanation seems insufficient or unconvincing, let them complete their thought before responding. This demonstrates respect and encourages them to be more open and honest in future conversations. Remember, the goal is to understand the motivations behind the lie, not just to punish the act itself.

Once you've heard their explanation, validate their feelings, even if you don't condone their actions. For example, if they lied about a poor grade to avoid disappointment, acknowledge their fear of letting you down. Saying something like, "I understand you were scared to tell me about your grade, but it's important to be honest with me, so we can work together to improve things" validates their feelings while still addressing the issue of dishonesty.

Restorative practices offer a powerful approach to addressing lying. Instead of focusing solely on punishment, these practices emphasize repairing the harm caused by the lie and restoring trust. This could involve having your preteen take responsibility for their actions, such as apologizing to the person they lied to or making amends for any damage caused. For example, if they lied about breaking something, having them help repair or replace the item instills a sense of responsibility and accountability.

Positive reinforcement plays a crucial role in discouraging dishonest behavior. Focus on rewarding honesty, no matter how small. When your preteen is truthful, even about challenging situations, praise their honesty and acknowledge their courage. This positive reinforcement creates a positive feedback loop, encouraging them to continue being truthful in the future. Avoid over-reliance on punishments, as this can create an environment of fear and distrust, making dishonesty more likely.

Building a strong parent-child relationship based on trust and open communication is essential in preventing and addressing dishonesty. This involves creating a safe space where your preteen feels comfortable sharing their thoughts and feelings without fear of judgment or punishment. Regular family meetings can provide a structured environment for discussing concerns, resolving conflicts, and fostering open communication. These meetings shouldn't feel like interrogations but should be opportunities for connection and open dialogue. During these meetings, encourage your preteen to voice concerns openly, ensuring you actively listen and respond thoughtfully, even if you disagree.

Consistency in your approach is vital. Setting clear expectations about honesty and consistently enforcing the consequences for dishonesty will help your preteen understand the importance of truthfulness. However, these consequences should always be proportional to the offense and focus on teaching responsibility rather than inflicting punishment. For instance, for a minor lie, a natural consequence might involve temporary loss of privileges. For more significant lies, more substantial consequences may be needed, always carefully considered and discussed with the child.

It's equally important to model honest behavior. Children learn by observing the adults in their lives. Be mindful of your own communication, ensuring that you're consistently honest in your interactions with your preteen and others. This demonstrates the value of honesty and creates a positive role model for your child to emulate. Be careful about making promises you can't keep, as this can undermine trust and create an environment where dishonesty seems more acceptable.

Address the root causes. Sometimes, lying might be a symptom of a deeper issue. If your preteen is consistently lying, consider whether there might be underlying emotional or psychological factors at play. This could include anxiety, depression, low self-esteem, or underlying learning difficulties. If you suspect an underlying problem, seeking professional help from a child psychologist or therapist is crucial. They can help identify and address these issues, leading to a more honest and open relationship with your child.

Remember, addressing lying isn't about winning a battle of wills, but about building a stronger relationship. By focusing on communication, restorative practices, and positive reinforcement, you can help your preteen develop a stronger moral compass and cultivate a more honest and open relationship. This is a process that takes time and patience, requiring consistent effort and understanding. The goal isn't just to stop the lying but to foster a deep sense of trust and open communication where your preteen feels safe being truthful. Celebrate small victories along the way and remember that setbacks are a part of the learning process. The journey to building an honest and trusting relationship requires patience, compassion and a commitment to understanding your preteen's perspective.

The consequences for dishonesty should be age-appropriate and consistently applied. For younger preteens, natural consequences, such as losing a privilege, might be sufficient. For older preteens, more significant consequences might be necessary, always explained clearly and calmly. However, punishment should never be the primary focus. The emphasis should always be on teaching responsibility and repairing the damage caused by the lie. This could involve making amends to the person who was lied to or taking on additional responsibilities to make up for the dishonesty. The goal is to help your preteen understand the impact of their actions and learn from their mistakes.

Involve your preteen in setting reasonable consequences for their actions. Collaboratively deciding on the consequences helps them understand the repercussions of their dishonesty and take ownership of the situation. This participatory approach also promotes a sense of responsibility and fairness, improving their understanding of accountability. This collaborative process fosters a sense of partnership and encourages them to actively participate in finding solutions to address their dishonesty.

It's crucial to differentiate between occasional lies and habitual dishonesty. Occasional lies, especially in younger preteens, may stem from immature judgment or a lack of understanding about the consequences of their actions. Consistent and persistent lying, however, can indicate a deeper underlying issue, such as low self-esteem, fear of punishment, or a need for attention. In such cases, seeking professional help from a child psychologist is recommended to explore potential underlying causes and develop strategies to address them.

Maintaining open communication is key to addressing lying effectively. Regular family meetings, informal conversations, and opportunities for sharing experiences contribute significantly to an environment of trust and openness. These interactions should be free of judgment and criticism, allowing your preteen to share their thoughts and feelings openly without fear of retribution. Active listening, validating their emotions, and demonstrating empathy are essential elements of these conversations.

Remember, honesty is a skill that develops over time. It requires consistent modeling, clear communication, and a supportive environment. By fostering a strong parent-child relationship based on trust and mutual respect, you can help your preteen develop the capacity for honesty and build a strong moral compass. Patience, understanding, and a consistent approach are key to guiding your preteen toward truthfulness and responsible behavior. It is a journey that involves ongoing effort and understanding, but the rewards of a trusting and honest relationship are immeasurable.

The transition into preadolescence often coincides with a period of increased experimentation and risk-taking. This is a natural part of development, as preteens begin to test boundaries, explore their independence, and navigate the complexities of their social world. However, some experimentation can lead to behaviors that pose significant risks to their physical and emotional well-being. It's crucial for parents to approach these situations with a combination of understanding, open communication, and proactive strategies. Addressing risky behaviors requires a delicate balance between setting firm boundaries and fostering a supportive environment where preteens feel comfortable discussing their challenges.

Substance use, including alcohol, tobacco, and drugs, is a serious concern during the preteen years. The influence of peers, media portrayals, and a desire to fit in can make preteens vulnerable to experimentation. Early intervention is key. Open and honest conversations about the risks associated with substance use should begin well before preteens are exposed to these substances. Educate your preteen about the potential consequences of substance use, focusing on the physical and mental health risks, the legal ramifications, and the impact on their relationships and future opportunities. It's essential to present this information without judgment or fear-mongering, creating a space where your preteen feels comfortable asking questions and expressing concerns.

Instead of resorting to lectures, frame your conversations around their interests and concerns. For example, if they're interested in sports, discuss how substance use can impair athletic performance. If they're concerned about social status, explain how substance use can damage their reputation and friendships. Tailoring your approach to their specific interests increases engagement and makes the conversation more relevant and relatable. It's also important to actively listen to their perspective, acknowledging their feelings and validating their concerns, even if you disagree with their choices.

Another critical aspect of addressing substance use is fostering strong family relationships. A preteen who feels loved, supported, and understood is less likely to engage in risky behaviors. Regular family dinners, activities, and open communication channels help create a strong foundation of trust and support. These interactions offer opportunities to reinforce family values, share experiences, and encourage open dialogue about difficult topics, including substance use. Remember, the goal is to build a strong, trusting relationship where your preteen feels comfortable approaching you with concerns or challenges.

Risky sexual behavior is another area that requires careful attention during preadolescence. Preteens are increasingly exposed to sexual content through media, social media, and peer interactions, making it essential to have open and age-appropriate conversations about sex, relationships, and sexual health. These conversations should begin early, focusing on healthy relationships, consent, and the importance of respecting boundaries. Open communication creates an environment where preteens feel comfortable asking questions and seeking guidance without judgment.

Avoid lecturing or resorting to fear-based tactics. Instead, approach the subject in a calm and informative manner, using age-appropriate language and resources. Explore the emotional and physical consequences of risky sexual behaviors, emphasizing the importance of personal responsibility and healthy decision-making. Provide accurate information about contraception, sexually transmitted infections, and the legal ramifications of sexual activity. Equip your preteen with the knowledge and skills they need to make informed choices about their sexual health.

Encourage open communication about relationships and dating. Help your preteen navigate the complexities of social dynamics, emphasizing the importance of healthy relationships built on mutual respect, trust, and communication. Teach them how to identify and avoid unhealthy relationships, including those that involve coercion, manipulation, or abuse. Empower your preteen to express their feelings, set boundaries, and seek help if they're experiencing an unhealthy relationship.

Self-harm, such as cutting, burning, or other forms of self-inflicted injury, is another serious concern during preadolescence. Often, self-harm is a coping mechanism for intense emotions, such as sadness, anger, anxiety, or stress. If you suspect your preteen is engaging in self-harm, approach the situation with empathy and understanding. Avoid judgment or criticism, focusing instead on creating a safe and supportive environment where they feel comfortable sharing their feelings.

Express your concern and willingness to help, emphasizing that they are not alone and that there are resources available to provide support. Encourage them to seek professional help from a therapist or counselor, who can provide guidance and strategies for managing their emotions and coping with difficult situations. In addition to professional support, consider family therapy, which can strengthen family bonds and facilitate communication about challenging topics.

Creating a safe space for communication is paramount in addressing all forms of risky behaviors. This involves fostering an environment of trust and respect, where your preteen feels comfortable sharing their thoughts and feelings without fear of judgment or punishment. Listen actively, validate their emotions, and provide reassurance that they are loved and supported. Encourage them to seek help if they're struggling, emphasizing that asking for help is a sign of strength, not weakness.

Access to appropriate resources and support networks is also crucial. Familiarize yourself with local mental health services, support groups, and online resources that can provide guidance and support to your preteen and your family. This proactive approach empowers you to provide prompt and effective assistance when needed. Remember, addressing risky behaviors requires a multifaceted approach that combines education, open communication, support, and access to appropriate resources. By fostering a strong parent-child relationship and creating a safe space for communication, you can guide your preteen toward making healthy and responsible choices. Early intervention and proactive strategies are vital in helping preteens navigate the challenges of this developmental stage and make safe, informed decisions about their well-being.

Early intervention is paramount in addressing these behaviors. The earlier you address risky behaviors, the better the chances of preventing escalation and long-term consequences. Don't wait for a crisis to occur before initiating conversations. Proactive discussions about healthy choices, boundaries, and the consequences of risky behaviors can lay the groundwork for open communication and support. Regular check-ins and opportunities for casual conversations can provide a natural pathway for addressing concerns without feeling like a formal interrogation.

Remember, parenting during preadolescence is a journey, not a destination. There will be ups and downs, successes and setbacks. Embrace the challenges, celebrate the victories, and remember that you are not alone. Utilize available resources, connect with other parents, and seek professional support when needed. Your preteen's well-being is a top priority, and investing time and effort in building a strong relationship and addressing potential risks is an investment in their future. The support of a therapist, counselor, or other mental health professional can provide invaluable guidance and tools to navigate these complex issues. Don't hesitate to seek professional assistance; it's a sign of responsible parenting, not a failure. The ultimate goal is to foster a thriving, healthy, and confident young person.

The journey of raising a preteen is rarely smooth sailing. While open communication and proactive parenting strategies form the bedrock of a healthy parent-child relationship, there will be instances when the challenges faced surpass the capacity of even the most dedicated parents. This is where seeking professional help becomes not just beneficial, but crucial. It's a sign of strength, not weakness, to acknowledge the need for external support and to actively seek it. Many parents hesitate, fearing judgment or believing they should be able to handle everything on their own. This misconception can delay intervention and potentially exacerbate the challenges faced by both the parent and the preteen.

Professional help can take many forms, each tailored to address specific needs. Therapy, for example, offers a safe and confidential space for preteens to explore their thoughts, feelings, and behaviors without judgment. A therapist can provide them with tools and strategies for managing difficult emotions, improving communication skills, and developing healthy coping mechanisms. For preteens struggling with anxiety, depression, or other mental health concerns, therapy can be transformative, providing guidance and support in navigating these complex emotions. The therapeutic process fosters self-awareness, helping preteens understand the underlying causes of their behaviors and develop healthier ways of responding to stressors. This understanding extends beyond the individual, positively influencing family dynamics and improving communication within the household.

Family therapy provides another avenue for support. It offers a structured environment where family members can address issues collectively, improving communication and fostering a stronger sense of unity. Family therapists facilitate open dialogue, helping families identify unhealthy patterns of interaction and develop healthier alternatives. This approach is particularly effective when dealing with challenging family dynamics, sibling rivalry, or conflicts arising from the preteen's behavioral challenges. The therapist acts as a facilitator, guiding family members towards improved understanding, empathy, and collaboration. The aim is to equip the family with the skills necessary to navigate future conflicts constructively and maintain a supportive and loving environment.

Counseling services offer a wider range of support, often encompassing both individual and family therapy. Counselors can address various issues, from academic struggles and peer pressure to substance abuse and risky behaviors. They provide guidance and support, helping preteens and families navigate the complexities of adolescence and make informed decisions about their well-being. Counseling may focus on developing coping skills, improving communication, and fostering self-esteem. The collaborative nature of counseling empowers both the preteen and the family, enabling them to actively participate in finding solutions and fostering positive change.

Identifying when professional support is needed can sometimes be challenging. There's no single checklist, but several warning signs indicate the need for intervention. Persistent disruptive behaviors that disrupt home life or school, significant changes in mood or personality, withdrawal from social activities and family engagement, a decline in academic performance, and self-harming behaviors are all cause for concern and warrant professional evaluation. Substance abuse, risky sexual behaviors, and expressions of suicidal ideation require immediate attention and professional intervention. Trust your instincts; if something feels off, don't hesitate to seek professional guidance.

Navigating the process of seeking professional help can feel overwhelming, but breaking it down into manageable steps can simplify the process. Start by researching therapists, counselors, or other mental health professionals in your area. Many insurance companies maintain provider directories, making it easier to locate professionals within your network. Online directories and professional organizations also provide valuable resources for finding qualified professionals. Consider factors such as specialization, experience, and therapeutic approach when selecting a professional. Reading reviews and testimonials from other clients can offer insights into a therapist's style and effectiveness.

The initial consultation serves as an opportunity to assess the fit between the family and the professional. During this meeting, discuss your concerns openly and honestly, allowing the professional to assess the needs of your preteen and your family. Ask questions about their approach to therapy or counseling, their experience working with preteens, and their fees and insurance coverage. Establishing a strong rapport with the chosen professional is crucial for the success of the therapeutic process. A comfortable and trusting relationship ensures open communication and cooperation from both the preteen and the family.

The frequency and duration of therapy or counseling sessions will depend on the specific needs and circumstances. Some preteens may benefit from short-term interventions focused on addressing specific issues, while others may require longer-term support for ongoing mental health concerns. The therapist or counselor will work collaboratively with the family to establish a treatment plan that aligns with the preteen's needs and goals. Regular communication between the therapist and parents is essential to ensure a cohesive and effective approach. This collaboration allows for consistent support and monitoring of the preteen's progress, enabling adjustments to the treatment plan as needed.

In addition to formal therapy and counseling services, various support systems can provide valuable assistance. Support groups connect parents and preteens with others facing similar challenges, fostering a sense of community and shared experience. These groups offer a platform for sharing experiences, coping strategies, and support, reducing feelings of isolation and promoting a sense of belonging. Many community organizations and schools offer parent support groups, providing a safe space to connect with others and access helpful resources. Online support forums and communities also offer valuable resources, allowing parents to connect with others from across geographical boundaries.

Educational resources, such as books, websites, and workshops, can provide valuable information and guidance. These resources can offer insights into adolescent development, communication strategies, and effective parenting techniques. They can equip parents with the knowledge and skills to better understand their preteen's behavior and develop more effective strategies for managing challenging situations. Schools often offer workshops and parenting classes, providing additional support and resources to families. Many online resources offer evidence-based information about adolescent development and parenting strategies.

Remember, seeking professional help is a proactive approach to ensuring your preteen's well-being. It's an investment in their future, fostering a stronger, healthier, and more resilient individual. Early intervention is often more effective and prevents the potential escalation of challenges. By acknowledging the need for external support and actively seeking it, you're demonstrating responsible parenting and prioritizing your preteen's well-being. The support of a professional can be transformative, providing the tools and strategies necessary to navigate the complexities of adolescence and foster a thriving parent-child relationship. Don't hesitate to reach out for help; it's a sign of strength and a testament to your commitment to your preteen's growth and well-being. The journey of parenting is a collaborative one, and accepting the need for professional guidance is a key step towards achieving the best outcome for your child.

Chapter 6:
Fostering Independence and Self-Esteem

The transition to preteen years marks a significant shift in a child's development, paving the way for increased independence and self-reliance. This journey, however, requires careful nurturing and guidance from parents. It's not about abruptly relinquishing control but rather about strategically empowering children to take on age-appropriate responsibilities, fostering their problem-solving skills, and cultivating a sense of ownership over their lives. This process is crucial for building self-esteem and preparing them for the challenges and opportunities of adolescence and beyond.

One of the most effective ways to foster self-reliance is through collaborative goal setting. Instead of dictating tasks or expectations, involve your preteen in the process. Sit down together and discuss realistic goals, considering their interests, abilities, and developmental stage. For example, instead of simply assigning chores, discuss with your child which household tasks they'd like to take responsibility for. Are they interested in helping with meal preparation, laundry, or yard work? Breaking down larger tasks into smaller, manageable steps can be particularly helpful for younger preteens who may feel overwhelmed by larger responsibilities. This collaborative approach fosters a sense of ownership and encourages commitment.

Once goals are established, create a visual aid to track progress, such as a chart or a whiteboard. This provides a tangible representation of their accomplishments, boosting their motivation and sense of accomplishment. Reward systems, however, should be approached thoughtfully. Focus on intrinsic rewards—the satisfaction of a job well done—rather than solely relying on extrinsic rewards, such as allowances or privileges. While monetary incentives can play a role, emphasizing the personal satisfaction derived from contributing to the family and accomplishing tasks is far more effective in cultivating long-term self-reliance. Celebrate successes, both big and small, praising their efforts and highlighting their growth. This positive reinforcement encourages them to continue striving for independence.

Teaching problem-solving skills is equally critical in fostering self-reliance. Preteens often encounter challenges that require them to think critically and creatively. Instead of immediately offering solutions, guide them through the process of identifying the problem, brainstorming potential solutions, evaluating the pros and cons of each option, and selecting the most effective course of action. This process teaches them valuable problem-solving skills that they can apply to various aspects of their lives. Real-life scenarios offer excellent opportunities for this type of learning. For example, if they lose a favorite toy, guide them through the steps of retracing their steps, searching thoroughly, and if the toy is still lost, discussing how they might cope with their disappointment.

Providing opportunities for children to learn from their successes and mistakes is integral to their development. Mistakes are inevitable, and they serve as valuable learning experiences. Instead of criticizing or punishing errors, approach mistakes as opportunities for growth. Help your preteen analyze what went wrong, what they could have done differently, and how they can avoid making the same mistake in the future. This approach fosters resilience, adaptability, and a growth mindset, essential qualities for developing self-reliance.

The balance between support and independence is a delicate act. While encouraging self-reliance is paramount, it is equally important to provide appropriate guidance and support. This doesn't mean shielding your preteen from challenges; instead, it involves offering support without taking over their responsibilities. Be available to offer advice, encouragement, and assistance when needed, but also allow them the space to navigate challenges on their own. This support system is crucial for building their confidence and fostering their belief in their abilities. Avoid micromanaging or constantly interfering; instead, provide encouragement and step in only when absolutely necessary.

Consistency is key when fostering independence. Establish clear expectations and routines, providing a sense of structure and predictability. This helps preteens feel secure and confident in their ability to manage their responsibilities. Avoid making exceptions to rules or constantly changing expectations, as this can create confusion and undermine their developing sense of self-reliance. Consistency provides a framework within which they can learn to take ownership of their actions and responsibilities.

Age-appropriate responsibilities are essential for developing self-reliance. Start with small tasks that align with their abilities and gradually increase the complexity and responsibility as they demonstrate competence. For example, younger preteens might start with tidying their room or setting the table, while older preteens might manage more involved chores, such as laundry or meal preparation. This gradual progression allows them to build confidence and develop a sense of accomplishment. It also helps them understand the importance of contributing to the family unit.

Open communication is the cornerstone of a healthy parent-child relationship. Create a safe and supportive environment where your preteen feels comfortable sharing their thoughts, feelings, and challenges. Actively listen to their concerns without judgment, offering encouragement and guidance without being overly critical. This open communication fosters trust and helps them understand that they can rely on your support when needed. Regular family meetings can be effective for open communication. These meetings can serve as a forum for discussing household issues, family plans, and individual concerns.

Beyond household chores, encourage self-reliance in other areas of their lives. For instance, teach them how to manage their time effectively, prioritize tasks, and plan their day. Encourage them to participate in extracurricular activities or hobbies that interest them, fostering their self-discovery and personal growth. Support their participation in group activities where they learn to collaborate with others, resolving conflicts peacefully and fostering teamwork. These experiences teach valuable life skills that extend beyond the immediate context.

In the academic sphere, encourage them to take ownership of their studies. Help them develop effective study habits, time management skills, and organizational strategies. Support them in setting academic goals and provide resources and guidance to help them achieve those goals. However, avoid doing their homework for them; instead, focus on teaching them the skills and strategies they need to be successful. This empowers them to manage their academic responsibilities independently, building their self-confidence and academic success.

The journey of fostering self-reliance is a gradual process that requires patience, understanding, and consistent effort. There will be setbacks and challenges along the way. It's important to remain supportive and encouraging throughout the process, remembering that building self-reliance is a marathon, not a sprint. By providing a supportive and structured environment, you equip your preteen with the skills and confidence they need to thrive, not only during their preteen years but also throughout their lives. Celebrate their achievements, acknowledge their efforts, and provide consistent guidance, creating a foundation for a confident, independent, and self-reliant individual. This journey is a shared endeavor, a collaborative effort between parent and child, fostering a strong and positive relationship based on mutual respect and understanding. The investment in fostering self-reliance is an investment in their future success and happiness.

Building a strong sense of self-esteem and confidence is paramount during the preteen years. This is a period marked by significant developmental changes, both physically and emotionally, and a child's self-perception can be profoundly impacted by these transitions. While fostering independence is crucial, it's equally important to equip preteens with the tools they need to navigate these challenges and develop a healthy sense of self-worth. This involves addressing common issues such as self-criticism, perfectionism, and negative self-talk, and providing them with the skills and support to cultivate a positive self-image.

One common hurdle is self-criticism. Preteens, particularly, can be incredibly hard on themselves, often magnifying minor flaws or setbacks. This critical inner voice can significantly impact their self-esteem and lead to anxiety and low self-confidence. It's essential to help them reframe their self-talk, shifting from negative and self-deprecating thoughts to more positive and encouraging ones. This doesn't involve ignoring their mistakes or shortcomings but rather helping them see these as opportunities for growth and learning, not indicators of personal failure. Encourage them to identify their strengths and focus on their accomplishments, however small. This positive reinforcement can gradually counteract the negative self-talk and help them build a more balanced and realistic self-perception.

Perfectionism is another significant challenge during these years. The desire to excel can be a positive motivator, but when it becomes an overwhelming need to be flawless, it can be detrimental to a child's mental and emotional well-being. Perfectionism often leads to excessive stress, anxiety, and avoidance of challenging tasks. It's crucial to help preteens understand that mistakes are an integral part of the learning process. Encourage them to embrace imperfection, to view challenges as opportunities for growth, and to strive for progress rather than unattainable perfection. Help them identify and challenge their perfectionistic thoughts, replacing unrealistic expectations with more realistic and attainable goals. This shift in mindset can significantly reduce stress and promote a more positive and confident approach to life.

Negative self-talk often manifests in the form of comparing themselves to others. Social media, peer pressure, and the inherent competitiveness of school can exacerbate this issue. Preteens may constantly compare their achievements, appearance, and popularity to those of their peers, often leading to feelings of inadequacy and low self-esteem. It is important to help them understand that everyone has unique strengths and weaknesses, and that comparing themselves to others is ultimately unproductive and detrimental to their self-worth. Encourage them to focus on their own progress and celebrate their individual achievements rather than measuring themselves against the accomplishments of others. This requires fostering a sense of empathy and self-compassion, helping them understand and accept their own individuality.

Building resilience is another critical component of fostering self-esteem. Resilience refers to the ability to bounce back from setbacks and challenges. Life inevitably presents difficulties, and teaching preteens how to navigate these obstacles with strength and determination is vital. This involves helping them develop coping mechanisms for stress, anxiety, and disappointment. This could include mindfulness exercises, problem-solving strategies, or simply having a supportive adult they can confide in. Encourage them to view challenges as temporary hurdles rather than insurmountable obstacles. Help them identify their internal strengths, their resources, and their support systems. By building their resilience, you equip them with the tools to overcome adversity and maintain a positive self-image even in the face of challenges.

Positive reinforcement is key in building self-esteem. Actively celebrate their achievements, no matter how small. Acknowledge their efforts, their persistence, and their growth. This positive reinforcement reinforces their sense of self-worth and motivates them to continue striving for their goals. This doesn't require extravagant rewards but rather genuine recognition and appreciation for their efforts. A simple "I'm proud of how hard you worked on that project," or "I noticed how much effort you put into that," can be far more impactful than a material reward. Focus on praising their effort and progress rather than solely focusing on the outcome. This fosters a growth mindset, encouraging them to see challenges as opportunities for learning and growth.

Helping preteens identify their strengths is crucial in building self-esteem. Encourage them to reflect on their talents, skills, and interests. This could involve engaging in activities that allow them to discover their strengths or exploring their passions through hobbies and extracurricular activities. Once they've identified their strengths, encourage them to utilize and develop those skills. This could involve taking on challenges that align with their strengths, seeking opportunities to showcase their abilities, or simply celebrating their unique talents. Understanding and appreciating their strengths helps them develop a more realistic and positive self-image.

Developing a healthy sense of self-acceptance is essential. This involves teaching preteens to accept themselves for who they are, including their flaws and imperfections. This doesn't mean being complacent or not striving for improvement but rather accepting their imperfections as part of what makes them unique. Encourage self-compassion, the ability to treat oneself with kindness and understanding, especially during difficult times. Model self-acceptance through your own behavior, showing them that it's okay to make mistakes and that it's important to forgive oneself. This fosters a healthy self-image, allowing them to focus on their positive attributes without being overly critical of themselves.

Fostering emotional well-being is closely linked to self-esteem. Teach preteens how to manage their emotions effectively, using healthy coping mechanisms to deal with stress, anxiety, and other challenging emotions. Encourage open communication about their feelings, creating a safe space where they feel comfortable expressing themselves without judgment. This might involve regular family discussions, journaling, or seeking support from a counselor or therapist. Emotional regulation skills are essential for navigating the challenges of adolescence and for building a strong sense of self-worth.

Open communication between parents and preteens is vital in building self-esteem. Create a safe and supportive environment where they feel comfortable expressing their thoughts and feelings without fear of judgment or criticism. Actively listen to their concerns, offering empathy and validation. Avoid dismissing their feelings or downplaying their experiences. This fosters trust and helps them understand that they are valued and supported. Regular family meetings can provide structured opportunities for open communication, allowing them to express their concerns and participate in family decision-making.

Involving preteens in decision-making processes empowers them and boosts their self-esteem. Give them choices and allow them some autonomy in making age-appropriate decisions. This could involve decisions about their clothes, extracurricular activities, or even household chores. This helps them develop decision-making skills, a sense of responsibility, and a belief in their ability to make positive choices. This sense of agency is crucial for building self-confidence and a healthy self-image. However, it is crucial to guide them, offer advice, and maintain appropriate boundaries.

The journey of building self-esteem is ongoing and requires consistent effort and support. There will be setbacks and challenges along the way. It's essential to maintain a supportive and encouraging approach, offering guidance and reassurance without being overly critical or controlling. Celebrate their progress, acknowledge their efforts, and focus on their strengths. By fostering a positive and nurturing environment, you can equip your preteen with the tools they need to develop a strong sense of self-worth, leading to greater confidence, resilience, and overall well-being. Remember, the ultimate goal is to nurture a healthy, confident, and self-assured individual ready to face the challenges and opportunities of life.

The journey toward independence isn't a straight path; it's a winding road filled with bumps, detours, and unexpected turns. A crucial aspect of guiding preteens toward self-esteem and autonomy involves fostering healthy risk-taking and building resilience. This delicate balance requires a shift in parental perspective, moving away from overprotective shielding to a more supportive, guiding role. It's about empowering preteens to navigate challenges, learn from mistakes, and develop the emotional fortitude to bounce back from setbacks. This isn't about abandoning caution; it's about calculated risk assessment, offering opportunities for growth within a framework of safety and support.

One of the most significant hurdles parents face is the fear of their child failing. This fear often stems from a desire to protect them from harm, both physical and emotional. However, the path to resilience is paved with mistakes and setbacks. Allowing preteens to experience age-appropriate risks, within carefully considered boundaries, is crucial for their development. This might involve letting them try out for a sports team despite the possibility of not making the cut, allowing them to attempt a challenging project even if it might not be perfect, or letting them navigate social situations independently, even if they might face rejection. The key is to strike a balance: offering support and guidance without hovering or excessively interfering.

Supporting a preteen's attempts at independence doesn't necessitate a complete absence of guidance. Instead, it involves providing scaffolding—support that gradually diminishes as their competence grows. This might involve offering advice and strategies, providing a listening ear, and offering encouragement when they falter. Instead of solving their problems for them, help them develop their own problem-solving skills. Ask open-ended questions that prompt critical thinking, such as "What are your options?" or "What are the potential consequences of each choice?" This empowers them to take ownership of their decisions and learn from the outcomes, positive or negative. The role shifts from being the solution-provider to being a facilitator, guiding them toward finding their own solutions.

Learning from mistakes is a fundamental aspect of growth. Instead of focusing on the error itself, emphasize the learning process. Help preteens analyze what happened, identify the contributing factors, and consider how they could approach similar situations differently in the future. Frame mistakes as opportunities for growth and learning, highlighting the valuable lessons gained from the experience. This approach shifts the focus from blame and punishment to reflection and improvement. Encourage them to view mistakes not as failures but as stepping stones on their journey toward competence. Ask questions like, "What did you learn from this experience?" or "How could you handle this differently next time?" This fosters a growth mindset, where challenges are viewed as opportunities for learning and development.

Developing problem-solving skills is a critical component of resilience. Equip preteens with the tools they need to approach challenges strategically. This involves teaching them various problem-solving techniques, such as brainstorming solutions, evaluating options, and making informed decisions. Role-playing scenarios can be invaluable in practicing problem-solving skills in a safe and controlled environment. By simulating real-life situations, preteens can develop their ability to think critically, anticipate consequences, and develop effective solutions. This practice strengthens their confidence and preparedness when faced with actual challenges. Furthermore, providing access to resources, like books, websites, or mentors, can further enhance their problem-solving capabilities.

Building emotional resilience is paramount in navigating the complexities of adolescence. This involves teaching preteens how to manage their emotions effectively, developing coping mechanisms to deal with stress, anxiety, and disappointment. This might involve teaching mindfulness techniques, such as deep breathing exercises or meditation, to help them regulate their emotional responses. Encouraging journaling can provide a valuable outlet for processing emotions and gaining self-awareness. Furthermore, promoting healthy lifestyle choices, such as regular exercise, a balanced diet, and sufficient sleep, can significantly improve emotional well-being and resilience. It is important to acknowledge that seeking professional help is not a sign of weakness, but rather a proactive step toward managing emotional challenges effectively.

The role of a supportive adult is indispensable in fostering resilience. Create a safe and nurturing environment where preteens feel comfortable expressing their vulnerabilities without fear of judgment or criticism. Be a reliable source of emotional support, offering empathy, understanding, and encouragement during challenging times. Teach them that it's okay to ask for help when needed and that seeking support is a sign of strength, not weakness. This open and trusting relationship provides a secure base from which they can explore new experiences and navigate setbacks with confidence. Building this strong foundation of trust and support enables preteens to feel confident in approaching challenges knowing they have a safety net in place.

The transition to adolescence is often accompanied by a heightened sense of self-consciousness. Preteens may become more sensitive to criticism and more susceptible to peer pressure. Supporting their self-esteem during this period requires a conscious effort to reinforce their strengths and validate their feelings. Focus on their individual talents and accomplishments, providing encouragement and positive reinforcement for their efforts. It is important to avoid making comparisons to siblings or peers, as this can undermine their self-confidence and lead to feelings of inadequacy. Instead, foster a sense of individual worth and celebrate their unique attributes. Encourage self-expression and independence, allowing them to develop their individuality within safe boundaries.

Establishing clear expectations and boundaries is crucial in fostering both independence and resilience. While granting preteens more autonomy, it's equally essential to maintain appropriate guidelines and expectations. This clear framework provides a sense of security and structure, enabling them to navigate the complexities of adolescence with confidence. The balance lies in allowing them to explore their independence while knowing there are established limits. These boundaries should be consistently enforced and communicated openly and transparently. This clarity helps them understand the expectations and feel secure within the established framework. Avoid overly restrictive rules that stifle their growth and development, opting instead for guidelines that promote responsibility and self-reliance.

Regular family discussions can provide opportunities for open communication and problem-solving. Creating a space where preteens feel comfortable sharing their thoughts and feelings without fear of judgment promotes emotional well-being and resilience. These discussions should focus on fostering collaboration and mutual understanding, rather than criticism or control. Actively listen to their concerns, validating their emotions and perspectives. By actively engaging in family dialogue, you create a stronger sense of connection and mutual support. This strengthens their sense of belonging and increases their willingness to seek guidance and support when needed. Remember, open communication is a two-way street, requiring active listening and genuine engagement from all parties.

Ultimately, fostering healthy risk-taking and building resilience involves a paradigm shift in parental approaches. Instead of solely focusing on preventing failures, we should focus on nurturing the skills and resilience needed to navigate inevitable challenges. This approach empowers preteens to become confident, self-reliant, and capable individuals equipped to face the opportunities and obstacles that life presents. The journey may involve setbacks and disappointments, but with consistent guidance, support, and a nurturing environment, preteens can develop the emotional strength and problem-solving skills needed to thrive. The outcome is the cultivation of self-assured, adaptable, and emotionally intelligent young adults ready to embrace the future with confidence and resilience. The rewards are far-reaching, impacting not only their self-esteem but also their overall well-being and success in life.

The groundwork for independence and resilience extends beyond simply allowing preteens to navigate challenges; it delves into cultivating a profound sense of purpose and meaning in their lives. This is not merely about achieving external success but about fostering an inner compass guiding them towards fulfilling activities and aspirations. Helping your preteen discover their passions and values forms a critical foundation for robust self-esteem and a resilient spirit. The journey begins with fostering self-discovery, a process of exploration and introspection that can be both exciting and challenging.

One effective approach is to encourage self-reflection through journaling. This doesn't require lengthy, philosophical entries; it can be as simple as prompting them to write down three things they enjoyed that day, what made them feel proud, or a challenge they overcame. These seemingly small exercises can illuminate recurring themes, revealing underlying interests and values. Regularly revisiting these journals can provide valuable insights into their evolving passions and priorities. Asking open-ended questions, such as "What activities make you feel truly engaged and energized?", "What are you naturally curious about?", or "What kind of impact do you want to make on the world?", can further stimulate self-exploration.

Actively participating in diverse activities is crucial for self-discovery. Expose your preteen to a wide range of experiences, from sports and arts to community service and academic clubs. This exploration allows them to identify their innate talents and preferences. It's not about forcing participation but about offering diverse opportunities within a supportive framework. If they express reluctance towards a particular activity, explore the reasons behind it. Perhaps it's the competitive nature of the activity, the social dynamics within the group, or a lack of perceived skill. Addressing these underlying concerns can unlock their potential and motivate participation.

Identifying strengths is an integral part of fostering a sense of purpose. It's easy to focus on weaknesses, but highlighting strengths boosts self-confidence and empowers preteens to embrace challenges. Observe your child's natural abilities and talents. Are they naturally empathetic? Do they possess exceptional organizational skills? Are they creative, technologically inclined, or perhaps possess remarkable leadership qualities? Affirming these inherent strengths builds confidence and creates a positive self-image, influencing their choice of activities and goals. This is not about creating an inflated sense of ego but about helping them recognize and leverage their natural gifts.

Once strengths are identified, encourage their development and application. If your preteen excels in writing, consider enrolling them in creative writing workshops or encouraging them to contribute to the school newspaper. If they have a knack for solving problems, encourage them to participate in robotics clubs or science fairs. Providing opportunities to develop and utilize their strengths in meaningful contexts fosters a sense of accomplishment and self-efficacy, bolstering their self-esteem and belief in their abilities. This connection between inherent strengths and meaningful activities strengthens their sense of purpose.

Supporting your preteen in setting meaningful goals is paramount. These goals shouldn't be imposed from the outside but should reflect their own aspirations and values. Engage them in a collaborative goal-setting process. Help them break down larger goals into smaller, manageable steps, making the process less daunting. Celebrate even the smallest successes along the way, recognizing and reinforcing their efforts. This process fosters perseverance, resilience, and a sense of accomplishment that fuels their motivation to continue striving toward their goals. Remember that the importance lies not only in achieving the goal itself but in the process of growth and learning along the way.

The pursuit of meaningful goals goes beyond individual accomplishments; it extends to making a positive contribution to society. Encouraging volunteer work or community involvement instills a sense of responsibility and social consciousness. This might involve volunteering at an animal shelter, participating in a local environmental cleanup, or assisting at a community center. These experiences offer valuable learning opportunities while instilling a sense of purpose beyond personal gain. The impact on their self-esteem is profound as they contribute to something larger than themselves. Witnessing the positive effects of their efforts strengthens their sense of self-worth and purpose.

Fostering a connection between their interests and their future aspirations is equally crucial. Discuss different career paths with your preteen, connecting their current interests to potential future opportunities. This doesn't require definitive career choices at this stage, but rather planting seeds of possibility. For instance, if your preteen enjoys drawing and design, discussing careers in architecture, graphic design, or fashion can broaden their horizons and encourage them to further explore these interests. This links their current activities to potential future pathways, creating a sense of direction and purpose.

Addressing setbacks and disappointments constructively is essential. The journey toward discovering and pursuing purpose is rarely smooth; it's characterized by challenges, failures, and moments of self-doubt. Help your preteen develop a growth mindset, emphasizing the value of learning from mistakes. Focus on the lessons learned rather than dwelling on the outcome. Encourage them to analyze what went wrong, identify areas for improvement, and approach the challenge with renewed perspective. This reinforces resilience, strengthens problem-solving skills, and prevents discouragement from derailing their pursuit of purpose.

The role of open communication cannot be overstated. Creating a safe and supportive environment where your preteen feels comfortable sharing their thoughts, feelings, and aspirations is paramount. Listen actively, validate their emotions, and offer guidance without judgment. Your unwavering support and understanding are essential in helping them navigate the challenges and uncertainties of self-discovery. Regular family discussions provide opportunities for meaningful dialogue and shared experiences, strengthening the bond and fostering a supportive network.

In conclusion, fostering a sense of purpose and meaning in a preteen's life is an ongoing process of exploration, self-discovery, and growth. It involves supporting their self-reflection, identifying their strengths, guiding them in setting meaningful goals, encouraging community involvement, and fostering open communication. The journey requires patience, understanding, and unwavering support. By empowering your preteen to discover their passions and pursue their goals, you equip them not only with the skills and resilience to navigate life's challenges but also with a profound sense of purpose and meaning, shaping them into confident, self-assured, and fulfilled individuals. This sense of purpose transcends mere self-esteem; it becomes the bedrock upon which a fulfilling and meaningful life is built. The investment in nurturing this inner compass yields immeasurable returns, impacting not only their adolescent years but shaping their trajectory for years to come. The strength and confidence derived from living a purposeful life are invaluable assets, providing resilience and motivation in the face of future obstacles.

The transition to adolescence marks a significant shift in a child's development, demanding a corresponding adjustment in parental strategies. While the foundational principles of open communication and mutual respect remain crucial, the methods of application need refinement to accommodate the evolving needs and emotional landscape of your teenager. Maintaining a strong, supportive relationship during this period hinges on understanding the unique challenges and opportunities that adolescence presents.

One of the most significant changes is the adolescent's increasing need for autonomy. This isn't a rejection of parental authority, but a natural developmental step towards self-reliance and independence. Parents need to carefully balance allowing their child greater freedom with maintaining necessary boundaries and guidance. This delicate balancing act requires consistent, clear communication. Avoid dictatorial pronouncements; instead, engage in collaborative discussions about expectations and consequences. For instance, instead of simply stating a curfew, involve your teen in setting a reasonable time, explaining the rationale behind it and allowing for some negotiation within acceptable parameters. This fosters a sense of responsibility and ownership, leading to greater compliance and a stronger parent-child bond.

Similarly, academic pressures intensify during adolescence, often accompanied by increased social demands. Maintaining open communication about schoolwork is paramount. Avoid interrogative questioning; instead, create an environment where your teen feels comfortable discussing academic challenges or triumphs. Ask open-ended questions such as, "How was your day at school?" or "Is there anything you're finding particularly difficult in your classes right now?" This approach encourages them to share their experiences and anxieties without feeling judged or pressured. Providing consistent support, whether it's helping with homework or simply offering a listening ear, reinforces your role as a reliable source of strength and guidance. Actively engage in their academic life – attend school events, communicate with their teachers, and show genuine interest in their learning process. This conveys your commitment to their academic success and affirms the importance you place on education.

The influence of peers becomes increasingly significant during adolescence, often leading to conflicts between peer expectations and family values. Understanding your teenager's peer group dynamics without resorting to judgmental labeling is critical. Avoid making sweeping generalizations about their friends; instead, encourage them to discuss their friendships, focusing on the positive aspects and addressing potential concerns with empathy and understanding. This allows you to build a trusting relationship, ensuring that they feel comfortable sharing potentially risky situations. This is not about controlling their friendships, but about equipping them with the critical thinking skills to navigate social pressures effectively and make sound judgments. Consider creating opportunities for social interaction within the family context – family game nights, outings, or even just relaxed conversations – to balance the influence of their peer group.

Another crucial aspect of the transition to adolescence is managing emotional fluctuations. Teenagers often experience intense mood swings, heightened sensitivity, and periods of emotional volatility. Recognizing that these changes are a normal part of adolescent development is key to navigating these turbulent waters effectively. Avoid dismissing their feelings as insignificant or trivial; instead, validate their emotions, emphasizing the importance of emotional expression. Creating a safe space where they can share their feelings without judgment is essential for maintaining a strong parent-child relationship. This doesn't mean endorsing every behavior, but rather understanding the underlying emotional drivers and responding with empathy and support. This empathetic response can include actively listening, acknowledging their feelings, and offering comfort or guidance as needed.

Navigating romantic relationships is another area requiring delicate parental guidance. The onset of romantic interests can lead to increased emotional intensity and potential anxieties. Open communication about healthy relationships is crucial. This includes discussions about respect, boundaries, consent, and the importance of safe and responsible behavior. Avoid lecturing or imposing strict rules; instead, encourage dialogue and share your own experiences and perspectives. This approach promotes critical thinking and equips your teen with the tools to make informed decisions about their relationships. Encourage them to discuss their relationships with you, creating an environment of trust and transparency.

Adolescence is also a time of significant physical changes. The hormonal shifts can result in changes in appetite, sleep patterns, and energy levels. Supporting your child through these changes requires understanding and patience. Openly discuss the physical changes they're experiencing, addressing their concerns with factual information and reassurance. Encourage healthy habits, such as regular exercise and a balanced diet, to mitigate the challenges of puberty. A supportive approach involves providing access to reliable health information and encouraging open discussions about body image and self-esteem.

Finally, encouraging continued participation in extracurricular activities and hobbies is vital for maintaining a well-rounded adolescent experience. Adolescence often presents a crossroads where extracurricular activities may be sidelined in favor of social activities or academic pressure. Open dialogue is crucial to prevent a complete abandonment of these pursuits. Actively supporting their existing interests and exploring new possibilities fosters a sense of identity and self-worth, providing outlets for creative expression and social interaction. This commitment to their pursuits demonstrates your faith in their abilities and your continued dedication to their growth.

The transition to adolescence is a journey, not a destination. It's a period of significant growth and change, demanding patience, understanding, and unwavering parental support. By embracing open communication, fostering a supportive environment, and adapting your parenting strategies to meet the unique challenges of this stage, you can help your child navigate this pivotal period with confidence and resilience, establishing a foundation for a strong and enduring relationship throughout their adult life. This period is not simply about managing behavior; it's about guiding your teen toward self-discovery, fostering autonomy, and ultimately, preparing them to become a responsible and well-adjusted adult. Remember that the goal is not to control their choices but to equip them with the skills and understanding to make healthy, informed decisions for themselves.

Chapter 7:
Maintaining Ongoing Positive Communication

The foundation of a strong and healthy parent-child relationship rests upon consistent and ongoing communication. This isn't merely about exchanging information; it's about fostering a deep connection built on mutual respect, understanding, and trust. While effective communication is crucial at all stages of a child's development, its importance intensifies during the preteen years, a period marked by significant physical, emotional, and social transformations. Maintaining open lines of communication during this phase lays the groundwork for a healthy and enduring relationship well into adulthood. It's a proactive investment in your child's well-being and future success.

Consistent communication goes beyond simply talking to your child; it necessitates active listening and genuine engagement. This means dedicating uninterrupted time to truly hear what your preteen is saying, both verbally and nonverbally. Notice their body language, their tone of voice, and the underlying emotions expressed, even if they aren't explicitly stated. Active listening demonstrates respect for their thoughts and feelings, creating a safe space for them to open up and share their experiences without fear of judgment or dismissal. This doesn't mean you have to agree with everything they say, but rather that you acknowledge and validate their perspectives. Simply showing that you are truly listening can make a world of difference in building trust and strengthening the parent-child bond.

Ongoing communication demands flexibility and adaptability. As your child grows and changes, your communication style should evolve as well. What worked when they were younger may not be as effective now. Preteens are developing their own identities and perspectives, and they need to feel heard and understood on their own terms. This means being receptive to their changing communication preferences, whether it's texting, emailing, or having face-to-face conversations. Respecting their preferred methods of communication demonstrates your willingness to meet them where they are and fosters a sense of connection. Don't be afraid to experiment with different approaches to find what resonates best with your child.

Creating opportunities for regular communication is also crucial. This doesn't have to be formal or structured; it can be as simple as having dinner together as a family, taking walks, or engaging in shared activities. These everyday moments create a natural flow of conversation and provide opportunities to connect on a deeper level. During these moments, focus on genuine interaction rather than lecturing or interrogating. Ask open-ended questions that encourage them to share their thoughts and feelings, and resist the urge to immediately offer solutions or advice. Sometimes, all they need is a listening ear and a feeling of being understood.

Consistency in communication involves establishing clear expectations and boundaries. These boundaries should be collaboratively determined, involving your child in the decision-making process. This allows them to feel a sense of ownership and control, leading to greater compliance and a stronger sense of responsibility. When setting boundaries, explain the rationale behind them clearly and calmly, allowing for negotiation whenever possible. Focus on positive reinforcement and acknowledge their efforts to follow the established rules. Punishments should be consistent and fair, and discussions about their consequences should involve open dialogue rather than arbitrary decisions.

Furthermore, consistent communication necessitates staying informed about your preteen's life. This involves actively participating in their activities, showing genuine interest in their hobbies, and staying connected with their teachers and school officials. Attend school events, communicate with their teachers regularly, and encourage them to share information about their academic progress and challenges. Demonstrate your involvement in their lives beyond just their academics; show interest in their friends, their social activities, and their personal interests. Staying connected in this way helps you understand their world better and allows you to offer support and guidance when needed.

Maintaining open communication extends beyond addressing challenges; it also encompasses celebrating successes, both big and small. Acknowledge their achievements, however minor they may seem. Celebrate their accomplishments and show pride in their efforts. This reinforces positive behavior and motivates them to strive for excellence. Expressing genuine appreciation for their hard work and dedication creates a positive and supportive environment where they feel valued and encouraged. Remember to praise effort as well as outcomes, fostering resilience and perseverance even when they face setbacks.

Beyond the immediate benefits of improved communication, the long-term effects are even more profound. Consistent and ongoing communication during the preteen years helps to build a strong foundation for future relationships. It equips them with essential communication skills, such as active listening, empathy, and conflict resolution, that will serve them well throughout their lives. This strong foundation will enable them to navigate the challenges of adolescence and beyond with greater confidence and resilience. The skills they learn in communicating with you will be transferable to their relationships with peers, teachers, and future partners.

A crucial aspect of ongoing communication is knowing when to seek professional help. Parenting is challenging, and sometimes, even the best communication strategies may not be enough. If you're struggling to connect with your preteen, if you're observing concerning behaviors, or if communication breakdowns seem insurmountable, don't hesitate to seek professional guidance from a therapist or counselor specializing in child and adolescent development. There's no shame in asking for help; it's a sign of strength and commitment to your child's well-being. A therapist can provide valuable insights and strategies to improve communication and address underlying issues that may be contributing to the challenges you're facing.

Finally, remember that communication is a two-way street. It requires effort and commitment from both you and your preteen. While you can create a supportive and communicative environment, your child also needs to actively participate in the process. Encourage them to express their thoughts and feelings, to ask questions, and to share their concerns. By fostering a culture of open dialogue and mutual respect, you create a strong and enduring bond that will serve as a source of support and guidance throughout their lives. The investment you make in consistent and ongoing communication will yield immeasurable rewards, shaping your child's emotional well-being and setting the stage for a positive and fulfilling future. The strength of your relationship during the preteen years can profoundly influence their ability to form healthy relationships throughout their adult life. This is not just about managing the challenges of this developmental phase; it's about building a lasting legacy of connection, trust, and mutual understanding. Remember, the goal is not merely effective communication, but the creation of a loving, supportive, and enduring bond.

As children transition through preadolescence and into adolescence, their communication styles and needs undergo a significant metamorphosis. What resonated yesterday might fall flat today, underscoring the critical need for parental adaptability. This isn't about abandoning previously successful strategies, but about refining and expanding them to meet the evolving complexities of your child's world. The key is to maintain relevance and connection, ensuring that your communication remains engaging, respectful, and effective throughout their development.

One of the most significant shifts occurs in the preferred methods of communication. Younger children readily engage in face-to-face conversations, often finding comfort in physical closeness. However, as children enter their preteen years, technology often becomes a dominant force. Texting, instant messaging, emailing, and social media platforms become preferred avenues for communication, offering a sense of anonymity and control that many preteens find appealing. While this might initially feel like a barrier to connection, it's essential to embrace these new channels as opportunities to engage. Responding promptly to their texts, acknowledging their emails, and showing a genuine interest in their online interactions demonstrates your willingness to connect on their terms. This doesn't mean abandoning face-to-face communication entirely, but rather integrating it with the methods they prefer. For instance, a quick text message acknowledging their day can be followed by a longer conversation at dinner.

The content of your conversations also needs to evolve. Topics that once held their full attention might now seem trivial. Preteens are grappling with complex issues – peer pressure, social dynamics, academic challenges, and the burgeoning awareness of their own identities. Their conversations will reflect these evolving concerns. It becomes crucial to listen actively, demonstrating genuine interest in their thoughts and feelings. Ask open-ended questions that encourage them to elaborate, avoid interrupting, and offer validating responses even if you don't necessarily agree with their perspectives. Avoid dismissing their feelings as "silly" or "dramatic," even if they seem so from an adult perspective. Validating their emotional experiences, no matter how small they may seem, builds trust and fosters open communication.

This shift necessitates a move away from the more directive communication styles often employed with younger children. Rather than lecturing or dictating, engage in collaborative conversations. Involve them in decision-making processes, offering choices and seeking their input on family matters. This empowers them, fostering a sense of autonomy and responsibility. For example, instead of dictating curfew times, engage them in a discussion about the rationale behind responsible time management and collaborate on a reasonable curfew that balances their needs with family expectations. This collaborative approach fosters a sense of partnership, creating a more positive and receptive communication environment.

The language you use also requires careful consideration. Avoid using patronizing or condescending language. Speak to them with respect, recognizing their growing capacity for critical thinking and independent thought. Use age-appropriate language, explaining complex issues in clear, concise terms. Avoid jargon or overly technical language that may confuse or alienate them. Instead, strive for open and honest dialogue, acknowledging that disagreements may arise, and that these differences of opinion are normal and healthy components of a strong relationship.

Remember that communication is bidirectional. It's not simply about imparting information; it's about actively listening and responding empathetically. Create spaces for them to share their perspectives without interruption or judgment. Even if their perspectives differ significantly from yours, demonstrating respectful listening validates their experience and builds trust. It's important to emphasize that open communication isn't about always agreeing; it's about fostering mutual understanding and respect even amidst disagreement.

Navigating conflicts is another crucial aspect of adapting communication strategies. Disagreements are inevitable, but the way these conflicts are handled significantly impacts the parent-child relationship. Avoid power struggles, seeking instead to resolve conflicts through collaborative problem-solving. Present your perspective calmly and rationally, listening actively to their point of view before proposing solutions. Encourage them to articulate their feelings and concerns without interruption, acknowledging their emotions even if you don't agree with their conclusions. Focus on finding mutually acceptable solutions, ensuring that both parties feel heard and respected.

The importance of maintaining consistent communication cannot be overstated. Regular check-ins, even short ones, demonstrate your commitment to the relationship and provide opportunities to address concerns before they escalate. These conversations don't need to be formal; casual chats during car rides, shared mealtimes, or even while engaging in shared activities provide natural openings for communication. These seemingly small moments of connection can accumulate, building a strong foundation of mutual understanding and support.

Adapting your communication style isn't a one-time event; it's an ongoing process requiring continuous adjustment and reflection. As your child's needs and interests evolve, so too must your communication strategies. Regularly assess the effectiveness of your approach, seeking feedback from your child when appropriate. Don't be afraid to experiment with different techniques to find what works best. The goal is to create a communication environment that is both comfortable and effective, fostering a strong and lasting bond.

Moreover, it is crucial to acknowledge the influence of the external environment on your child's communication and behavior. Peer pressure, academic demands, and social media usage can significantly impact their emotional state and their interactions with you. Stay informed about their experiences in these areas, demonstrating a genuine interest in their lives beyond academics. Engage in discussions about their friends, their social activities, and their online experiences. This demonstrates your involvement in their world, creating a space for open and honest dialogue about the challenges and triumphs they face. This also gives you a better understanding of the context that shapes their actions and communication styles.

Consider the impact of cultural and individual differences on communication styles. Not all children communicate in the same way. Some are more verbal, while others may express themselves more through actions or written communication. Understanding your child's individual communication preferences is key to fostering effective interactions. Respect their preferred methods of communication, whether it's through conversations, texts, emails, or other means. Acknowledge their unique communication style and tailor your approach accordingly.

The role of technology in modern communication also requires careful consideration. While technology provides new opportunities for connection, it also introduces potential challenges. Excessive screen time can negatively impact communication, potentially hindering face-to-face interactions and creating a sense of emotional distance. Establish healthy boundaries around technology use, ensuring that technology doesn't become a barrier to meaningful communication. Encourage activities that foster face-to-face interaction, such as family dinners, games, or outdoor activities, to counterbalance screen time.

Finally, remember that seeking professional help is a sign of strength, not weakness. If you're struggling to connect with your child, if communication breakdowns are frequent or severe, or if you're observing concerning behaviors, don't hesitate to seek guidance from a therapist or counselor specializing in child and adolescent development. They can provide valuable insights and strategies to improve communication and address underlying issues that may be contributing to the difficulties.

Adapting communication strategies as children mature is an ongoing journey, not a destination. It requires continuous effort, flexibility, and a commitment to understanding your child's evolving needs. By embracing these changes and adapting your communication approaches accordingly, you can foster a strong, loving, and enduring bond that will serve them well throughout their lives. The investment in understanding and adapting communication strategies is an investment in the future wellbeing and success of your child.

Building a strong parent-child relationship is the cornerstone of effective communication and a child's healthy development. It's not simply about talking; it's about creating a deep, lasting connection built on trust, mutual respect, and unconditional love. This bond provides a secure base from which children can explore the world, tackle challenges, and develop a strong sense of self. It's a relationship that evolves and adapts as your child grows, requiring consistent effort, empathy, and a willingness to learn and adapt.

One crucial aspect of building this strong relationship is fostering a sense of security and safety. Children need to know that they can come to you with anything, without fear of judgment or punishment. This means creating a non-judgmental space where they feel comfortable sharing their thoughts, feelings, and experiences, even the difficult ones. This doesn't mean condoning negative behaviors, but rather providing a safe environment to discuss them openly and constructively. Imagine a scenario where your preteen is struggling with a friend; instead of immediately dismissing their feelings, create a space for them to express their frustration and hurt. Ask open-ended questions like, "Tell me more about what happened," or "How did that make you feel?" Active listening, showing empathy, and validating their feelings are key. Avoid interrupting or offering unsolicited advice until they have fully expressed themselves. This approach shows them that their feelings are valid and worthy of attention.

Creating a consistent routine also contributes significantly to building a secure attachment. Regular family meals, shared activities, and dedicated time for one-on-one interaction are essential. These shared experiences foster bonding and provide opportunities for natural conversation. Family dinners, for example, don't need to be formal affairs; they can be informal gatherings centered around conversation and connection. Even short interactions, like a quick chat before bed or a walk together after school, provide opportunities to connect and check in on their day. These small moments accumulate, building a reservoir of positive interactions that strengthen the parent-child bond.

Beyond shared activities, it is vital to actively participate in your child's life. Show a genuine interest in their hobbies, friends, and school experiences. Attend their school events, sporting matches, or musical performances. Engage in conversations about their day, asking specific questions about their classes, friendships, and activities. This shows them that you value their experiences and are invested in their overall well-being. This active participation extends to their online activities as well. While monitoring their online interactions is important, doing so with respect and trust helps maintain open communication. Avoid overly restrictive measures, and focus instead on open conversations about internet safety, online interactions, and responsible technology use. The goal is not to control their digital interactions, but to guide them in making safe and responsible choices.

Another critical element is demonstrating unconditional love and acceptance. This means loving and accepting your child for who they are, regardless of their mistakes or shortcomings. This doesn't equate to condoning negative behaviors, but it does involve providing consistent support and understanding, even during challenging times. Criticizing them for mistakes or expressing conditional love – "I'll love you only if..." – can significantly damage the parent-child relationship. Instead, focus on praising their efforts and progress, even in areas where they struggle. Celebrate their accomplishments, both big and small, and offer consistent encouragement during setbacks. This creates a secure base where they feel loved and accepted, regardless of their imperfections.

Furthermore, empowering your child through shared decision-making fosters a sense of autonomy and responsibility. Involve them in age-appropriate choices and decisions that affect their lives. Instead of making decisions for them, give them options and guide them through the decision-making process. For instance, instead of dictating their clothing choices, give them options within reasonable limits. Or involve them in planning family outings or meals.

This approach cultivates a sense of ownership and responsibility, fostering independence and self-confidence.

Open communication isn't solely about imparting information; it's a two-way street. It involves actively listening to your child's perspective, understanding their feelings, and validating their experiences. Even if you disagree with their perspective, actively listen and validate their emotions before offering your own insights. This active listening goes beyond just hearing their words; it means paying attention to their body language and tone of voice. Emphasize the importance of expressing feelings constructively, showing them healthy ways to communicate anger, frustration, or sadness. Modeling appropriate conflict resolution skills is also crucial; show them how to handle disagreements calmly and respectfully.

Conflict is inevitable in any relationship, and the parent-child relationship is no exception. However, how you navigate conflict significantly impacts the overall relationship. Avoid power struggles; instead, strive for collaborative problem-solving. Frame disagreements as opportunities for learning and growth, emphasizing mutual respect and understanding. Engage in calm, respectful conversations, ensuring that both parties feel heard and valued. The goal isn't to "win" the argument, but to reach a mutually agreeable solution.

Building a strong parent-child relationship is an ongoing process, requiring consistent effort and a willingness to adapt to your child's evolving needs. It's a journey, not a destination. Regularly assess the effectiveness of your communication and strategies, seeking feedback from your child when appropriate. Be willing to adjust your approaches and find what works best for both of you. The reward—a strong, loving, and enduring bond—is invaluable. It provides a foundation for your child's emotional well-being, fostering resilience, self-esteem, and a strong sense of self. This investment in your relationship with your child is an investment in their future success and happiness. Remember that seeking professional guidance is a sign of strength, not weakness. If you encounter significant challenges in communication or observe concerning behaviors, don't hesitate to seek support from a therapist or counselor specializing in family dynamics and child development. They can provide valuable insights and tools to enhance your relationship and address any underlying issues.

Celebrating your preteen's successes, no matter how small, is crucial for fostering their self-esteem and motivation. This isn't about showering them with material gifts; it's about acknowledging their effort, perseverance, and growth. A simple "I'm so proud of how hard you worked on that project," or "I noticed you really persevered with your piano practice," can have a profound impact. These affirmations validate their efforts and encourage them to continue striving for excellence. Remember to focus on the process, not just the outcome. Even if they didn't achieve a perfect score on a test or win the competition, praising their dedication and commitment reinforces their intrinsic motivation. For instance, if your child diligently practiced for a school play but didn't land a lead role, praise their commitment to rehearsals and the improvement in their acting skills. This approach focuses on their growth and effort, rather than solely on the outcome.

Beyond verbal praise, consider more tangible ways to celebrate achievements. A special family dinner, a trip to their favorite place, or a small, meaningful gift can reinforce the importance of their accomplishments. The key is to tailor the celebration to their individual interests and preferences. If they achieved a personal best in a sporting event, a celebratory dinner at their favorite restaurant might be ideal. If they excelled in a school project, perhaps a special family movie night is appropriate. The aim is to create positive associations with their accomplishments, making them more likely to strive for future successes. The celebrations don't have to be elaborate; even small gestures, like a heartfelt card or a special dessert after dinner, can make a big difference.

However, navigating the preteen years inevitably involves facing challenges. Academic struggles, social difficulties, and emotional upheavals are all part of this developmental stage. Your role as a parent is not to shield your child from these difficulties, but to equip them with the resilience and coping mechanisms to navigate them successfully. This involves providing a supportive and understanding environment where they feel comfortable sharing their struggles without fear of judgment. Instead of immediately offering solutions, create space for them to express their emotions and thoughts. Ask open-ended questions like, "Tell me more about what's happening," or "How are you feeling about this?" Active listening demonstrates empathy and validates their emotions. Remember, sometimes just being present and listening without offering advice can be incredibly powerful. They need to know that they are heard and understood, even if you don't fully comprehend their perspective.

Supporting your preteen through challenges doesn't mean fixing their problems for them. Instead, it involves guiding them toward finding their own solutions. Encourage them to brainstorm potential solutions and weigh the pros and cons of each option. Help them identify their strengths and resources, empowering them to take ownership of their challenges. For instance, if they are struggling with a difficult assignment, help them break it down into smaller, more manageable tasks. If they are having trouble making friends, explore strategies for building social connections, such as joining clubs or participating in extracurricular activities. The goal is not to eliminate the challenges they face, but to help them develop the skills and confidence to overcome them independently.

Furthermore, it's vital to differentiate between supporting and rescuing. While offering guidance and support is essential, avoid rescuing them from every difficulty. Allowing them to experience the natural consequences of their actions, within safe limits, helps them learn valuable life lessons and develop problem-solving skills. For example, if they miss a deadline for a school project due to procrastination, help them understand the consequences and develop strategies for better time management in the future. This process fosters responsibility and accountability, essential life skills that extend far beyond the preteen years. However, this doesn't mean neglecting their emotional needs. Ensure that they know you are there to support them emotionally, even when they face the consequences of their choices.

Another crucial aspect of supporting your preteen through challenges involves teaching them healthy coping mechanisms. This might include strategies for managing stress, such as practicing mindfulness, deep breathing exercises, or engaging in physical activity. Encourage them to express their feelings through creative outlets like writing, drawing, or music. These activities can provide healthy outlets for expressing emotions and processing difficult experiences. Moreover, promoting a healthy lifestyle – regular sleep, balanced nutrition, and physical activity – significantly impacts their emotional and mental well-being. These habits provide a strong foundation for coping with stress and navigating life's inevitable challenges. Explain the connection between physical health and mental well-being, emphasizing the importance of self-care.

Recognizing that some challenges might require external support is also vital. If your preteen is experiencing persistent difficulties, don't hesitate to seek professional help. A therapist or counselor specializing in adolescent development can provide valuable guidance and support for both your child and your family. This isn't a sign of failure as a parent; it demonstrates a proactive approach to ensuring your child's well-being. They can offer evidence-based strategies to address specific issues, providing tools and techniques to navigate challenging situations. Remember, seeking professional help is a sign of strength, not weakness. It signifies a commitment to your child's emotional and mental health, ensuring they receive the support they need to thrive.

Throughout this process, maintaining open communication remains paramount. Regular check-ins, family dinners, and shared activities provide opportunities for casual conversations and connection. These informal moments often reveal underlying issues or anxieties that might not be apparent during formal discussions. Active listening and empathy remain crucial, creating a safe space where your preteen feels comfortable sharing their thoughts and feelings without judgment. This approach helps build trust and strengthens the parent-child bond, fostering resilience and promoting open dialogue even amidst challenging circumstances. Remember, open communication isn't a one-time event; it's a continuous process requiring patience, understanding, and consistent effort.

Furthermore, consider your own emotional well-being. Parenting preteens is demanding, and it's easy to become overwhelmed by the challenges they face. Prioritizing your own self-care – through exercise, relaxation techniques, or pursuing personal interests – is not selfish; it's essential for effective parenting. Taking care of yourself allows you to be more present and supportive for your child. This includes seeking support from your own network – friends, family, or support groups – when you need it. Remember, you are not alone in this journey, and seeking support is a sign of strength, not weakness.

Finally, remember that celebrating successes and supporting through challenges is a collaborative process. Involve your preteen in finding solutions to problems and celebrating accomplishments. This fosters a sense of shared responsibility and empowers them to take ownership of their life. This collaborative approach strengthens the parent-child bond, building trust and mutual respect. It teaches valuable life skills, fostering resilience, independence, and a strong sense of self. The journey of parenting a preteen is challenging but incredibly rewarding. By fostering open communication, celebrating successes, and offering unwavering support during challenging times, you create a strong foundation for your child's emotional well-being and future success. Remember, this is a journey, and by focusing on the relationship and working together, you can navigate the complexities of the preteen years successfully.

This section aims to equip you with a comprehensive list of resources to further support your journey in navigating the complexities of raising a preteen. The challenges of this developmental stage are significant, and having access to reliable information and support networks can make a world of difference. Remember, seeking help is a sign of strength, not weakness, and utilizing these resources demonstrates your commitment to your child's well-being.

We'll begin with online resources. The internet offers a wealth of information, but it's crucial to be discerning about the sources you consult. Look for reputable websites affiliated with established organizations or universities. Websites of professional organizations like the American Psychological Association (APA) and the American Academy of Pediatrics (AAP) offer evidence-based articles and resources on child development, parenting, and adolescent psychology. Their websites frequently feature articles and information specifically addressing the challenges of preteen development, providing practical advice and coping strategies for parents. Many articles delve into specific issues parents often face, such as managing screen time, dealing with peer pressure, or navigating academic struggles.

Beyond professional organizations, numerous parenting websites provide valuable insights and support. However, always critically evaluate the information presented, looking for evidence-based practices and avoiding sites that promote unsubstantiated or potentially harmful approaches. Look for websites that cite their sources and are written by qualified professionals in the field of child development or psychology. Many websites offer forums or online communities where parents can connect with others facing similar challenges, fostering a sense of shared experience and mutual support. These online communities can provide invaluable emotional support and practical advice from other parents who have navigated similar situations.

Moving beyond online resources, consider the wealth of knowledge available in books. Libraries and bookstores offer a vast selection of parenting books catering specifically to the challenges of raising preteens. Look for books written by child psychologists, developmental pediatricians, or other qualified professionals in related fields. These books often provide research-based strategies and practical guidance on various aspects of preteen development, such as communication, discipline, and emotional regulation. When selecting books, pay attention to the author's credentials and the book's overall tone. Opt for books that offer practical advice, evidence-based strategies, and a supportive, encouraging approach to parenting. Avoid books that promote overly punitive or restrictive parenting styles.

Local community resources often play a vital role in supporting families. Many communities offer parenting classes and workshops led by experienced professionals. These classes provide an opportunity to learn from experts, connect with other parents, and gain valuable insights into effective parenting strategies. Check with your local library, community center, school district, or healthcare provider for information on available parenting classes and support groups. The benefits of attending these classes extend beyond acquiring knowledge; they offer a chance to connect with other parents facing similar challenges, fostering a sense of community and mutual support. Sharing experiences and advice with other parents can be incredibly valuable in navigating the ups and downs of raising preteens.

In addition to parenting classes, consider exploring local support groups specifically designed for parents of preteens. These groups offer a safe and supportive environment where parents can share their experiences, concerns, and challenges without judgment. The sense of community and shared understanding these groups provide can be invaluable in reducing feelings of isolation and helplessness. Many organizations, such as YMCA's, churches, community centers, and hospitals, often offer support groups. Check local listings or contact your pediatrician or family doctor for referrals to local support groups for parents of preteens and adolescents.

When considering professional services, remember that seeking help from a therapist or counselor is not a sign of failure; it is a proactive step towards ensuring your child's well-being. A therapist specializing in adolescent development can provide invaluable guidance and support for your child and your family. They can assess your child's individual needs and provide evidence-based therapies and interventions to address specific challenges. If you are facing significant difficulties in communicating with your preteen or are struggling to manage challenging behaviors, a therapist can offer strategies and coping mechanisms to help improve your interactions and strengthen your family relationships.

Finding a suitable therapist can sometimes be challenging. Start by asking your pediatrician, family doctor, or school counselor for referrals. You can also search online directories of therapists specializing in adolescent development or family therapy. When choosing a therapist, consider factors such as their experience, approach to therapy, and personality. It's important to find a therapist with whom you feel comfortable and confident. The therapeutic relationship is crucial for effective treatment, so selecting a therapist who creates a safe and supportive environment for your child is essential.

In addition to therapists, family counselors can play a significant role in supporting families facing complex challenges. Family counselors offer a space for open communication and conflict resolution within the family unit. They can facilitate constructive dialogue, help improve family dynamics, and teach healthy communication skills. Family counseling is particularly helpful when dealing with issues such as sibling rivalry, conflict between parents and children, or family stress related to a child's behavioral or emotional challenges. The collaborative nature of family counseling empowers family members to work together to identify solutions and improve their relationships.

Beyond therapeutic services, consider seeking guidance from educational psychologists or school counselors if your preteen is struggling academically or socially at school. These professionals can assess your child's learning style, identify learning disabilities or social-emotional challenges, and develop strategies to support their academic and social success. They can also work with teachers and school staff to ensure your child receives appropriate support and accommodations within the school environment. Early intervention is crucial for addressing academic and social difficulties, and working with educational psychologists or school counselors can significantly improve your child's overall school experience.

This comprehensive list of resources offers numerous avenues to support your journey in parenting your preteen. Remember, you are not alone in this process. Utilizing these resources demonstrates your commitment to fostering a healthy and supportive environment for your child, equipping them with the tools and resources they need to thrive during this critical developmental stage. By combining the strategies and advice from this book with the resources listed above, you can create a strong foundation for open communication, mutual respect, and a loving parent-child relationship. This journey is challenging, but with consistent effort and the right support, you can successfully navigate the complexities of the preteen years and cultivate a strong and lasting bond with your child. Remember, the ultimate goal is to guide your child towards becoming a responsible, independent, and emotionally well-adjusted young adult, and utilizing these resources is a crucial step towards achieving this goal.

www.ingramcontent.com/pod-product-compliance
Lightning Source LLC
Chambersburg PA
CBHW071248130626
46556CB00003B/1222